BOOK OF LOFTS
LE LIVRE DES LOFTS
DAS LOFTBUCH

BOOK OF LOFTS
LE LIVRE DES LOFTS
DAS LOFTBUCH

EVERGREEN

© 2009 EVERGREEN GmbH, Köln

Editors:
Simone Schleifer, Julio Fajardo

English translation:
Matthew Clarke

French translation:
Marion Westerhoff

German translation:
Susanne Engler

Copy editing:
Cristina Doncel

Art director:
Mireia Casanovas Soley

Graphic design and layout:
Ignasi Gracia, Anabel Naranjo

Printed in China

ISBN 978-3-8365-1151-3

Contents Sommaire Inhalt

The origins of lofts can be traced back to the New York of the 1950s: at that time, artists and bohemians in search of cheap places to live and work began to move into abandoned late-nineteenth-century industrial buildings. These iron-framed premises were once the site of garment sweatshops, furniture companies, printmaker shops, warehouses, depositories, and factories. As industries moved away from Manhattan to cheaper areas, these buildings became vacant. Artists seized this low-cost opportunity to create a new American version of the Parisian artist's atelier and began moving into these spaces. As such, they unknowingly created what we now refer to as the loft.

Nowadays, the tendency to convert warehouses and factories into homes has extended everywhere, creating a style that can be applied to all types of spaces and inhabitants. What were once large, spartan shells, often occupied illegally by students and artists with limited financial means, have grown into elegant, luxurious residences reserved for a wealthy elite or premises for professionals who require a place in which they can both live and work. The common denominators are large, open areas with no dividing walls or partitions, floor-to-ceiling windows, and an extraordinary amount of natural light. Exposed materials from the original building—steel and wood, for example—allude to an industrial aesthetic and a marriage between old and new adapted to the needs and tastes of the occupants. A recent (and flourishing) trend in loft design reflects a move away from transforming old factory buildings toward the conversion of conventional dwellings, using the loft approach to take advantage of their spatial and functional flexibility. New materials and design techniques have produced a generation of lofts that have become sophisticated and highly prized assets.

This book provides examples that illustrate how this trend is applied today, from huge industrial spaces to small premises where architects have to take the fullest possible advantage of the spatial possibilities to create a feeling of greater expansiveness. The ideas come from some of the most renowned architects in the world, and they can be applied to a variety of spaces and interpreted in different ways to suit personal tastes and satisfy specific requirements.

L'origine des lofts remonte au New York des années 50 : à cette époque, artistes et bohèmes en quête de logements et d'ateliers bon marché, commencèrent à s'installer dans des bâtiments industriels abandonnés de la fin du XIXᵉ siècle. Autrefois, ces structures d'acier hébergeaient des ateliers de vêtements, des fabriques de meubles, des imprimeries, des entrepôts, des garde-meubles et des usines. Tous ces bâtiments furent délaissés lorsque les industries quittèrent Manhattan pour des quartiers moins chers. En s'installant dans ces locaux désaffectés très bon marché, les artistes profitèrent de cette véritable aubaine pour créer la version américaine des ateliers d'artistes parisiens. Sans le savoir, ils fondèrent ce que nous appelons aujourd'hui un loft.

De nos jours, la tendance à transformer entrepôts et usines en logement s'est généralisée un peu partout, créant un style adapté à un large éventail d'espaces et de personnes. Les grandes structures austères de jadis, souvent occupées de manière illégale par des étudiants et des artistes démunis, se sont métamorphosées en résidences élégantes et luxueuses, devenues l'apanage d'une élite aisée ou de professionnels en quête d'un lieu alliant domicile et bureau. Ces habitations ont de nombreuses caractéristiques communes : espaces ouverts sans murs ni cloisons, baies vitrées tout en hauteur et lumière du jour à profusion. La structure initiale apparente des bâtiments d'origine – mariant souvent l'acier et le bois – rappelle l'esthétique industrielle et l'alliance entre l'ancien et le moderne, adaptée aux besoins et goûts des occupants. La tendance récente (et florissante) du design de loft est en train de changer de cap : la restauration d'anciennes usines cède le pas à la reconversion de logements conventionnels, appliquant les critères de modulation de l'espace et des fonctions caractéristiques du loft. Les nouveaux matériaux et les récentes techniques de design ont engendré une nouvelle génération de lofts superbes, très en vogue.

Ce livre regorge d'exemples illustrant la tendance actuelle, dans un éventail allant d'immenses espaces industriels à de petits logements où les architectes ont optimisé les données spatiales pour exalter l'impression de largesse. Les idées présentées sont issues des plus prestigieux architectes du monde. Modulables selon les espaces, elles peuvent s'interpréter de mille et une façons, au gré des goûts et des besoins de chacun.

Die Ursprünge der Lofts liegen im New York der 1950er-Jahre: Damals begannen Künstler und Bohemiens auf der Suche nach günstigen Räumen zum Wohnen und Arbeiten, in verlassene Industriegebäude aus dem späten 19. Jahrhundert zu ziehen. Die Gebäude auf den von Eisenzäunen umgebenen Geländen beherbergten einst Textilmanufakturen, Möbelfabriken, Druckereien, Lagerhäuser, Depots und andere Betriebe. Seitdem die Betriebe nach und nach begonnen hatten, von Manhattan weg in billigere Zonen zu ziehen, standen die Gebäude leer. Künstler nutzten diese Gelegenheit und zogen in die kostengünstigen Gebäude, um eine amerikanische Version der typischen Pariser Ateliers zu kreieren. Damit schufen sie, ohne es zu wissen, das, was wir heute Loft nennen.

Heute ist der Trend, ehemalige Lagerhäuser und Fabrikgebäude in Wohnhäuser umzuwandeln, weit verbreitet und erstreckt sich auf alle Arten von Räumen und Bewohnern. Was einst großflächige, spartanische Räume waren, oft illegal besetzt von Studenten und Künstlern mit begrenzten finanziellen Mitteln, sind heute elegante, luxuriöse Wohnungen, die einer wohlhabenden Elite vorbehalten sind, oder Wohn- und Arbeitsräume von gut verdienenden Freischaffenden. Geblieben sind die großen, offenen Bereiche ohne Mauern oder Trennwände, die hohen Fenster vom Boden bis zur Decke und die außergewöhnlich hohe Menge an natürlichem Licht. Offen liegende Baumaterialien der ursprünglichen Gebäude wie Stahl und Holz sorgen für eine Industrieästhetik und eine Verbindung von Alt und Neu, die zu den Anforderungen und dem Stil der neuen Bewohner passt. Ein neuer und florierender Trend beim Entwurf von Lofts geht weg von der Umwandlung alter Fabrikgebäude hin zur Neugestaltung von herkömmlichen Wohnungen, wobei die räumliche und funktionelle Flexibilität des Loftdesigns genutzt wird. Innovative Materialien und Designverfahren haben eine neue Generation von ausgefeilten Lofts geschaffen, die zu hoch geschätzten Immobilienwerten geworden sind.

In diesem Buch werden Beispiele dargestellt, die zeigen, wie dieser Trend heute umgesetzt wird. Es werden riesige Industriegebäude, aber auch relativ kleine Räume vorgestellt, bei denen die Architekten alle räumlichen Möglichkeiten bis ins Letzte ausnutzen mussten, um den Raum größer wirken zu lassen. Die Entwürfe zu den hier vorgestellten Lofts stammen von einigen der renommiertesten Architekten der Welt. Sie sind für eine Vielzahl von Gebäuden geeignet und können auf verschiedene Weise interpretiert werden, um an stilistische und andere spezielle Anforderungen angepasst zu werden.

Structural Loft

Attilio Stocchi
Bergamo, Italy

Given the extraordinary height of the ceilings here, the architect decided to take advantage of the space and incorporate an additional level. The loft is articulated around thirteen steel posts scattered over the space in asymmetrical clusters. These posts support the system of horizontal planes to create a sensation of instability, arbitrarily piercing whatever comes in their way. The public zone was allocated to the lower level, while the private zones were lifted onto the upper structures. Two slanted posts puncture an oval glass dining table and continue through a floating structure with a bathroom suspended from the ceiling. The steel posts in the bedroom are both structural and decorative. Another key element is the intricate steel sculpture situated underneath a glass panel in the ground floor, which shines at night. The pervasive use of steel creates a distinctive style and a sense of continuity within the loft.

Dans cet espace, bénéficiant d'une hauteur de plafond extraordinaire, l'architecte a décidé d'optimiser l'espace en y incorporant un niveau supplémentaire. Le loft s'articule autour de treize piliers d'acier répartis dans l'espace en groupes asymétriques. Ils soutiennent le système de plans horizontaux afin de créer une sensation d'instabilité, traversant au hasard tout ce qui croise leur chemin. La zone publique est située au niveau inférieur tandis que les sphères privées sont élevées au niveau des structures supérieures. Deux piliers élancés crèvent une table de verre ovale et traversent ensuite une structure flottante dotée d'une salle de bains suspendue au plafond. Les colonnes d'acier de la chambre à coucher sont structurales et décoratives. Une sculpture d'acier complexe, autre élément clé, se trouve sous un panneau de verre au rez-de-chaussée qui brille la nuit. L'omniprésence de l'acier crée un style particulier et imprime l'intérieur du sceau de la continuité.

Aufgrund der außergewöhnlichen Deckenhöhe baute der Architekt eine weitere Ebene ein. Das Loft wird von dreizehn in asymmetrischen Gruppen über den Raum verteilten Stahlpfosten gegliedert. Diese Pfosten stützen das System horizontaler Ebenen, das ein Gefühl von Instabilität entstehen lässt und willkürlich alles durchsticht. Der öffentliche Bereich befindet sich unten, während die privaten Räume auf den oberen Ebenen liegen. Zwei schräge Pfostenstruktur durchbohren einen Esstisch aus Glas und werden durch eine schwebende, an der Decke hängende Struktur, in der sich ein Badezimmer befindet, weitergeführt. Im Schlafzimmer dienen die Stahlpfosten sowohl als Struktur- als auch als Dekorationselemente. Ein anderes Schlüsselelement ist die Stahlskulptur unter der Glasplatte im Erdgeschoss, die nachts beleuchtet ist. Das Vorherrschen des Materials Stahl schafft einen besonderen Stil und sorgt für Kontinuität in allen Räumen.

The use of glass to protect the catwalk ensures transparency and the flow of light throughout both levels of the loft.

L'emploi du verre, pour protéger la passerelle, dote l'espace de transparence et assure la fluidité de la lumière sur les deux niveaux du loft.

Durch den Einsatz von Glas zum Abschirmen des Stegs wurde große Transparenz erreicht, und das Tageslicht kann in beide Ebenen des Lofts eindringen.

› Section Section Schnitt

› Plan Plan Grundriss

The intricate steel sculpture is another key element of the design. It shines at night and creates a distinctive effect, giving a sense of continuity within the loft.

Une sculpture d'acier complexe est aussi un élément clé de l'espace. Elle brille la nuit, créant un effet particulier qui imprime l'intérieur du loft du sceau de la continuité.

Ein anderes Schlüsselelement dieses Projektes ist die ausgefallene Stahlstruktur. Nachts leuchtet sie und schafft eine einzigartige Atmosphäre innerhalb des Lofts.

The steel pillars frame the bed from behind, serving as both structural and decorative elements.

Les piliers d'acier surplombent le lit et font à la fois partie de la structure et du décor.

Die Stahlpfosten, die direkt hinter dem Bett zusammenlaufen, haben sowohl strukturierende als auch dekorative Funktion.

The upper level consists of glass walkways that lead to the bedroom and bathroom.

Le niveau supérieur est constitué de passerelles de verre qui mènent à la salle de bains en marbre et à la chambre à coucher.

Die obere Etage besteht aus verglasten Stegen, die zu dem Marmorbadezimmer und dem Schlafzimmer führen.

Loft in A Coruña

A-cero

A Coruña, Spain

A once dark and divided space was converted into a loft-style residence by tearing down the existing partitions and introducing a series of pivoting panels. The existing mezzanine was preserved and modified slightly around the staircase, while the hall was stripped to provide a greater sense of space in the entrance. The column that previously supported the mezzanine was replaced by a tension rod to relieve the perception of heaviness. Stairs recessed in the wall lead to an upper level that houses the bedroom, bathroom, and dressing room. The public areas and domestic functions are divided by small differences in levels or materials on the floor and ceiling. A translucent glass balcony subtly divides the two levels and provides seclusion for the private areas. The furnishings, from the picture frames to the armchairs, were designed as a part of the project and include a complex kitchen module that contains all the appliances and bathroom elements.

Cet espace, autrefois sombre et cloisonné, est reconverti en une résidence de style loft. Les parois sont remplacées par une série de panneaux pivotants. La mezzanine préexistante et conservée dans ce projet, est légèrement modifiée autour de l'escalier. Le hall d'entrée est mis à nu pour accroître la sensation d'espace. Dans un souci de légèreté, la colonne qui, au départ, soutenait la mezzanine, est remplacée par un câble tenseur. L'escalier, encastré dans le mur, mène à l'étage supérieur, vers la chambre, la salle de bains et le dressing. La séparation entre les zones publiques et les zones privées est marquée par des différences de niveaux ou de matériaux de revêtement du sol et du plafond. Un balcon en verre transparent divise délicatement les deux niveaux, tout en assurant l'intimité des sphères privées. L'aménagement intérieur, allant des encadrements de tableaux aux fauteuils, à été conçu l'instar du module complexe de la cuisine entièrement équipée et dotée d'éléments de salle de bains.

Dieser ehemals dunkle und enge Raum wurde in eine Wohnung im Loftstil umgebaut. Dazu wurden Trennwände eingerissen und schwenkbare Paneele konstruiert. Das Zwischengeschoss blieb erhalten und wurde im Treppenbereich leicht verändert. Der Flur wurde vollständig von allen einengenden Elementen befreit, um im Eingangsbereich den Eindruck von Großzügigkeit zu erzielen. Eine Zugstange ersetzt die Säule und lässt so die Konstruktion leichter wirken. Treppen in einer Wandnische führen zur oberen Ebene, wo sich Schlafzimmer, Bad und Ankleidezimmer befinden. Die öffentlichen und häuslichen Bereiche sind durch leichte Höhenunterschiede oder verschiedene Decken- und Fußbodenmaterialien voneinander getrennt. Eine lichtdurchlässige Glasgalerie teilt die beiden Ebenen und sorgt für Privatsphäre. Der Entwurf der Möbel, von den Bilderrahmen bis zu den Sesseln, war Teil des Projektes; dazu gehörten auch ein komplettes Küchenmodul mit allen Geräten und die Badezimmerelemente.

The furnishings were designed as a part of the architectural project and the stairs were recessed in the wall; they lead to an upper level that houses the bedroom, bathroom, and dressing room.

L'ameublement s'inscrit dans la conception du projet d'architecture et l'escalier, encastré dans le mur, mène à l'étage supérieur, vers la chambre, la salle de bains et le dressing.

Der Entwurf des Mobiliars war Teil des architektonischen Gesamtentwurfs. Die Treppe ist in einer Aussparung in der Wand untergebracht und führt in die obere Etage, wo sich Schlafzimmer, Badezimmer und Ankleidezimmer befinden.

› Ground floor Rez-de-chaussée Erdgeschoss

› First floor Premier étage Erstes Obergeschoss

Gray Loft

Work AD
New York, United States

The aim was to convert this loft on the eleventh floor of a building in the center of Manhattan into a home with three bedrooms, four bathrooms and a spacious living room suitable for large-scale social occasions. The design was preconditioned by the existence of two terraces and 23 windows distributed along three of the four façades, so it was decided that the layout would not break up this perimeter. So, the rooms are placed in the center of the home and are encircled by floating walls, providing an appearance of graceful lightness. The living room is an unbroken open space in which floor coverings and rugs mark off the different spaces for watching television, relaxing, listening to music or socializing with friends. The kitchen, made of stainless steel and Corian, has been placed in the southeast corner, in order to take advantage of the morning sun.

L'idée était de convertir ce loft, situé au onzième étage d'un édifice, au centre de Manhattan, en un logement comportant trois chambres, quatre salles de bains et un salon spacieux pour de grandes réceptions. Le design devait tenir compte de l'existence de deux terrasses et de 23 fenêtres distribuées sur trois des quatre façades. Il fut donc décidé de garder ce périmètre. De ce fait, les pièces sont regroupées au cœur de l'habitation et entourées de murs flottants, conférant à l'ensemble une impression de gracieuse légèreté. Le salon est un espace totalement ouvert et fluide uniquement séparé par les tapis qui délimitent ainsi les différentes zones : télévision, détente, musique ou rencontre. Pour profiter du soleil matinal, la cuisine, en acier inoxydable et en Corian, a été installée dans l'angle sud-est.

Dieses Loft im 11. Stockwerk eines Gebäudes im Zentrum von Manhattan sollte zu einer Wohnung mit drei Schlafzimmern, vier Badezimmern und einem großen Wohnzimmer umgebaut werden, in dem größere Zusammenkünfte möglich sind. Bei der Planung musste berücksichtigt werden, dass es zwei Terrassen und 23 Fenster an drei der vier Fassaden gab, die erhalten werden sollten. Deshalb wurden die Räume in die Mitte der Fabriketage gesetzt und von mobilen Wänden umgeben, wodurch das Loft sehr hell wirkt. Das Wohnzimmer ist ein vollständig offener Raum, in dem Fußbodenbelag und Teppiche die verschiedenen Bereiche zum Fernsehen, Entspannen, Musik hören oder Freunde treffen markieren. Um von der Morgensonne zu profitieren, befindet sich die Küche aus Edelstahl im Südosten der Wohnung.

The large plasma-screen television is placed on a pivoting stand so that it can be conveniently turned and viewed from different points in the living room.

L'immense écran plasma, placé sur un socle pivotant, peut être dirigé au gré des besoins et vu depuis divers endroits du salon.

Der riesige Plasmafernseher befindet sich auf einem schwenkbaren Möbel, das in alle Richtungen des Wohnzimmers gedreht werden kann.

› **Plan** **Plan** Grundriss

The leftover spaces, where the Corian wall approaches the façades, are used as dressing-rooms, small storerooms, or makeshift guest rooms.

Les parties restantes, à l'endroit où le mur en Corian rejoint les façades, font office de dressing, de petits débarras ou de chambre d'amis improvisée.

Die übrigen Räume, in denen sich die mit Corian verkleideten Wände der Fassade annähern, werden als Ankleidezimmer, Abstellkammern oder behelfsmäßige Gästezimmer benutzt.

Carlo Donati
Milan, Italy

Loft A

This space was originally a traditional Milanese house with a balustrade, divided into two small apartments, one on the top floor and the other on the bottom floor, connected to a spacious area which served as an art gallery. After a radical refurbishment, a spiral staircase was put in between the first and second floors, where the bedrooms are located. The rooms on the first floor have interior and exterior spaces and receive direct sunlight. They include the kitchen, which acts as a filter between the entrance and the rest of the house. The electrical system provides maximum flexibility in the lighting, which was a basic premise of the project. The architectural and structural concepts were largely determined by the materials used. Some structures are made of carbon fiber and whole swathes of the floor are covered with a resin. The original parquet floor was only retained in the bedroom.

Jadis une maison milanaise traditionnelle dotée d'un balcon, cet espace était divisé en deux petits appartements, un à l'étage et l'autre au niveau inférieur, reliés à une large pièce servant de galerie d'art. Suite à une restauration d'envergure, un escalier en colimaçon a été installé entre les deux étages où se trouvent les chambres à coucher. Les pièces situées au premier étage, dotées d'espaces intérieur et extérieur, reçoivent la lumière du jour directe à l'instar de la cuisine qui sert de filtre entre l'entrée et le reste de la maison. Le système électrique permet un éclairage complètement modulable, idée directrice du projet. Les matériaux employés sont déterminants dans le concept architectural de l'ensemble. Certaines structures sont en fibres de carbone et dans son ensemble, le revêtement du sol est en résine. Seul le parquet de la chambre à coucher est d'origine.

Dieses Haus war einst ein traditionelles mailändisches Gebäude mit Balustrade. Es wurde in zwei kleine Wohnungen im Ober- und Erdgeschoss aufgeteilt, die durch eine weitläufige Kunstgalerie verbunden sind. Nach einer radikalen Sanierung wurde eine Wendeltreppe zwischen dem ersten und dem zweiten Stockwerk, in dem sich die Schlafzimmer befinden, eingebaut. Die Räumlichkeiten der ersten Etage verfügen über innere und äußere Räume und erhalten direktes Sonnenlicht. Die Beleuchtung ist durch ein spezielles elektrisches System sehr flexibel, was eine der Grundvoraussetzungen dieser Planung war. Die architektonischen und strukturellen Konzepte sind stark von den eingesetzten Materialien bestimmt. Manche Strukturen bestehen aus Kohlenstofffaser, und stellenweise ist der Fußboden harzbeschichtet. Das Originalparkett ist nur noch im Schlafzimmer zu finden.

Natural light illuminates the lower floor and brightens up the corridor. The ramp of the stairs also receives sunshine thanks to the insertion of a window situated above it.

La lumière naturelle illumine l'étage inférieur et éclaire le couloir. La rampe des escaliers reçoit aussi les rayons de soleil grâce à une fenêtre insérée juste au-dessus.

Tageslicht dringt in das Untergeschoss und den Korridor. Auch die Treppe erhält durch ein oben liegendes Fenster Licht von außen.

The dining room is a spacious room characterized by functionality, while also providing open spaces for leisure to foster the social use of the room.

La salle à manger spacieuse se caractérise par sa fonctionnalité. Elle est également dotée d'espaces ouverts pour les loisirs, accentuant la fonction sociale de la pièce.

Das Esszimmer ist ein großer, funktioneller Raum, der sehr offen wirkt und als Treffpunkt dient.

› **Ground floor** Rez-de-chaussée Erdgeschoss

› **First floor** Premier étage Erstes Obergeschoss

The materials used are an important part of the architectural and structural concept. Some structures are made of carbon fiber and the flooring is covered with a resinous material.

Le choix des matériaux employés est un critère important du concept architectural et sculptural. Certaines structures sont en fibres de carbone et les sols sont recouverts de résines.

Die verwendeten Materialien sind ein wichtiger Bestandteil des architektonischen und strukturellen Konzeptes. Einige der Strukturen bestehen aus Kohlenstofffaser, der Boden ist mit einem Harz beschichtet.

› Longitudinal section Section longitudinale Längsschnitt

Samarcanda stone is used in the design of the bathroom. It is part of the relaxation area and was designed to be integrated into the living-room area.

Le design de la salle de bains a été réalisé en pierre de Samarkand. Elle fait partie de la zone de relaxation. Sa conception l'intègre au salon.

Das Badezimmer ist mit dem Naturstein Samarcanda ausgestattet. Es gehört zur Entspannungszone und ist so angelegt, dass es in den Wohnbereich integriert ist.

Hunter Ritaco Loft

Ruhl Walker Architects
Boston, United States

The owners assigned Ruhl Walker Architects to design the complete interior of their residential loft and they desired total openness and flexibility, with all the spaces flowing together as freely as possible with multiple domestic, socializing and business functions. The pre-existing, long, windowless side walls are activated by modulations of the new ceiling planes and custom millwork on one side, and a virtual 'floating window' of steel and translucent, back-lit acrylic on the other. This translucent wall, the loft's main source of light, opens up to become a home office at one end and conceals the dressing-room at the other. Large concealed sliding doors allow the owners to reconfigure the spaces to accommodate constantly fluctuating needs for privacy. The flooring is charcoal-gray stained maple in the main spaces, honed green limestone in the master bathroom, and black slate in the entrance and guest bathroom.

Les propriétaires ont chargé le bureau d'études Ruhl Walker Architects du design de tout l'intérieur de leur loft résidentiel, selon les critères spatiaux suivants : ouverture totale, flexibilité, fluidité, liberté maximale et fonctions multiples domestiques, sociales et professionnelles. Les longs murs latéraux préexistants, dépourvus de fenêtres, sont activés par de nouveaux plafonds en panneaux modulables et un mécanisme d'engrenage sur un côté. Une « fenêtre flottante » virtuelle en acier et acrylique translucide rétro-éclairé s'inscrit de l'autre côté. Ce mur translucide, source de lumière principale, s'ouvre et se métamorphose, d'un côté, en bureau, et de l'autre, dissimule le dressing. Grâce à de grandes portes coulissantes intégrées, le propriétaire peut reconfigurer l'espace au gré de ses besoins d'intimité. Le sol des espaces principaux est en érable ponctué de gris charbon, en grès vert vif dans la salle de bains du propriétaire et en ardoise noire dans l'entrée et la salle de bains des amis.

Die Kunden beauftragten Ruhl Walker Architects mit dem Entwurf des gesamten Lofts. Sie wünschten sich offene, multifunktionale Räume, die privaten wie sozialen und gesellschaftlichen Ansprüchen genügen sollten. Die bereits vorhandenen fensterlosen Seitenwände wurden durch Modulationen der neuen Deckenplatten und Holzfertigplatten auf einer Seite und dem virtuellen „schwebenden Fenster" aus Stahl und lichtdurchlässigem, von hinten beleuchtetem Acryl auf der anderen Seite belebt. Die lichtdurchlässige Wand, die als Hauptlichtquelle dient, öffnet sich zu einem Heimbüro auf der einen Seite und verbirgt das Ankleidezimmer auf der anderen. Große verdeckte Schiebetüren machen es möglich, die Räume flexibel zu gestalten und die individuell gewünschte Privatsphäre zu schaffen. Der Fußboden ist in den Haupträumen mit dunkelgrauem Ahorn und im Hauptbadezimmer mit grünem, polierten Kalkstein belegt. Im Eingangsbereich und den Gästebadezimmern findet man schwarzen Schiefer.

The owners desired total openness and flexibility, combined with a range of materials that would enhance these general aims and stimulate the senses.

Les propriétaires voulaient une ouverture et une flexibilité totales, alliées à un éventail de matériaux renforçant cet objectif et stimulant les sens.

Der Eigentümer wünschte sich eine offene und veränderbare Umgebung, kombiniert mit einer Vielzahl von Materialien, die diese Wirkung noch unterstreichen und die Sinne anregen.

› Plan Plan Grundriss

Large, concealed sliding doors allow the owners to reconfigure the spaces to accommodate the constantly fluctuating needs for privacy.

De grandes portes coulissantes escamotables permettent aux maîtres des lieux de remodeler l'espace au gré des fluctuations de leur besoin d'intimité.

Große verdeckte Schiebetüren ermöglichen eine flexible Raumgestaltung und schaffen Privatsphäre.

Multimedia Studio

Agnes Blanch, Elina Vila/
Minim Arquitectos
Barcelona, Spain

The loft was created for a multimedia artist whose colorful works are design elements that bring vitality to the space. The interior designers' philosophy springs from their perception of minimalism as a series of concepts that value simplicity, austerity, and elegance, rather than a passing aesthetic trend. The kitchen became the center of attention; a free-standing island with a stainless-steel countertop faces the living area, flanked by a wall of closets. A partition conceals the bedroom and stops short of the ceiling to favor the entrance of light. In the bedroom, an original sculpture serves as a decorative and practical coat-hanger. The bathroom is set behind a half-height stone wall that does not obscure the high windows and the structural columns, while the light materials used inside contrast with these solid structures. The counter seems to float between the two columns, while the glass basin rests lightly on top of it.

Le loft a été créé pour un artiste du multimédia dont les œuvres de design colorées ravivent l'espace. La philosophie du designer est de percevoir le minimalisme davantage comme une série de concepts valorisant la simplicité, la sobriété et l'élégance plutôt qu'une tendance esthétique éphémère. La cuisine centralise l'attention : un îlot unique recouvert d'inox fait face au salon, flanqué d'un mur de placards. Une cloison masque la chambre à coucher et s'arrête peu avant le plafond pour laisser passer la lumière. Dans la chambre à coucher, une sculpture originale à la fois décorative et pratique, fait office de portemanteau. La salle de bains se love derrière un mur de pierre à mi-hauteur, laissant ainsi filtrer la lumière des fenêtres hautes sans pour autant cacher les colonnes structurales. Les matériaux légers de l'intérieur contrastent avec ces structures solides. Le plan des toilettes semble flotter entre les deux colonnes avec l'évier de verre posé délicatement dessus.

Dieses Loft wurde für einen Multimediakünstler geschaffen, dessen bunte Arbeiten die Räume beleben. Grundlage der Gestaltung war ein minimalistisches Konzept, das auf Werten wie Einfachheit, Nüchternheit und Eleganz beruht und kein vorübergehender ästhetischer Trend ist. Die Küche bildet in diesem Loft den Mittelpunkt, eine freistehende Insel, die dem Wohnbereich, begrenzt von einer Wand voller Wandschränke, gegenüberliegt. Ein Raumteiler, der nicht ganz bis zur Decke reicht, sodass noch Licht einfällt, trennt das Schlafzimmer ab. Im Schlafzimmer dient eine originelle Skulptur als dekorativer und praktischer Kleiderständer. Das Badezimmer befindet sich hinter einer halbhohen Steinmauer, die die hohen Fenster und Säulen nicht verdeckt. Die leichten Materialien im Badezimmer bilden einen Gegensatz zu diesen festen Strukturen. Der Waschtisch, auf den sich ein leichtes, gläsernes Waschbecken stützt, scheint zwischen zwei Säulen zu schweben.

The loft was created for a multimedia artist whose colorful works endow the space with life.

Le loft a été créé pour un artiste du multimédia dont les œuvres de design, hautes en couleur, ravivent l'espace.

Das Loft wurde für einen Multimediakünstler entworfen, dessen bunte Werke es mit Leben füllen.

The kitchen became the center of attention; a free-standing island with a stainless steel countertop faces the living area, which is flanked by a wall covered with closets.

La cuisine monopolise l'attention : un îlot central doté d'un comptoir en inox fait face au salon, flanqué d'un mur de placards intégrés.

In diesem Loft bildet die Küche den Mittelpunkt. Der Wohnbereich befindet sich, begrenzt von einer Wand voller Wandschränke, gegenüber.

In the bedroom, an original sculpture serves as a decorative but practical coat-hanger. A partition conceals the bedroom and stops short of the ceiling to enhance the entrance of light.

Dans la chambre à coucher, une sculpture originale, décorative et pratique à la fois, fait office de portemanteau. Une cloison masque la chambre et s'arrête peu avant le plafond pour laisser filtrer la lumière.

Im Schlafzimmer dient eine originelle Skulptur als dekorativer und praktischer Kleiderständer. Ein nicht ganz bis zur Decke reichender Raumteiler trennt das Schlafzimmer ab, ermöglicht aber den Einfall von Tageslicht.

Light materials like wood and glass were used in the bathroom, which is situated behind a half-height stone wall and preserves the view of the tall windows and the structural columns.

Des matériaux légers, tel le verre, sont utilisés dans la salle de bains, située derrière un mur de pierre à mi-hauteur, préservant la vue sur les hautes fenêtres et les colonnes structurales.

Im Badezimmer wurden leichte Materialien wie Holz und Glas verbaut. Es liegt hinter einer halbhohen Steinmauer, und man sieht von dort aus noch die großen Fenster und die Säulen der Struktur.

Loft in Milan

Patrizia Sbalchiero
Milan, Italy

Formerly a carpenter's workshop, these premises were transformed into a living space for a couple of young graphic designers and their child. The loft is characterized by high ceilings that consist on one side of wooden beams and on the other of metal sheets. The architect chose to divide the vertical space into two and insert a mezzanine level, accessed by a steel and wood staircase, which leads to the studio (slightly taller than the remaining space). The pitched glass ceiling was layered with bamboo screens and draped with white fabric to diffuse the direct sunlight, which, in turn, is filtered through two glass panels in the floor into the dining-room area directly below. Downstairs, the living space looks onto the bright orange kitchen and dining area that contrasts strikingly with the antique table and chairs. The decoration in the child's bedroom was created by her mother and creates an atmosphere of magic and fantasy.

Atelier de charpentier par le passé, cet endroit a été transformé en un espace de vie pour un couple de jeunes graphistes et leur enfant. Ce loft se distingue par de hauts plafonds parés d'un côté de poutres de bois et de l'autre, de plaques de métal. L'architecte a pris le parti de diviser l'espace vertical en deux et d'y intégrer une mezzanine reliée par un escalier d'acier et de bois menant au studio (légèrement surélevé par rapport au reste de l'espace). Le haut plafond de verre est habillé de paravents en bambous et drapés de tissu diffusant la lumière directe du soleil, filtrée, tour à tour, par deux sols en verre, dans l'espace de la salle à manger située juste en dessous. En bas, le salon donne directement sur la cuisine et la salle à manger orange vif, contrastant ainsi avec les chaises et la table anciennes. La décoration de la chambre d'enfant, empreinte de magie et de fantaisie, est l'œuvre de la mère.

Diese einstige Schreinerwerkstatt wurde in ein lebendiges Zuhause für ein Paar, beide Grafikdesigner, und deren Kind umgestaltet. Das Loft hat hohe Decken, die auf einer Seite aus Holzbalken und auf der anderen aus Metallplatten bestehen. Der Architekt beschloss, den vertikalen Raum in zwei Bereiche zu unterteilen und ein Zwischengeschoss einzuziehen, das man über eine Treppe aus Stahl und Holz erreicht. Diese führt ins Atelier (etwas größer als der restliche Raum). Die geneigte Glasdecke ist mit Bambusrahmen und weißem Stoff bedeckt, um das direkte Sonnenlicht zu zerstreuen, das dann durch die beiden Glasfußböden bis in den darunter liegenden Essbereich dringt. Der Essbereich und die Küche in lebendigem Hellorange liegen dem Wohnbereich gegenüber und kontrastieren stark mit der antiken Sitzgruppe. Die magische und fantastische Atmosphäre des Kinderzimmers entstand durch die Dekoration, die die Mutter selbst entworfen hat.

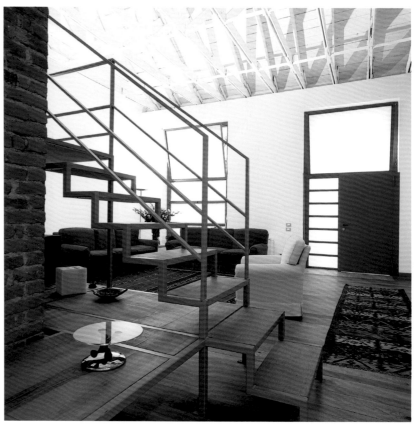

The metal structure incorporates a table-like surface that helps to accentuate the unity of the two levels.

La structure en métal comprend une surface plane qui permet de souligner l'unité entre les deux niveaux.

Die Metallstruktur bildet eine Oberfläche, die einem Tisch gleicht und eine Verbindung zwischen den beiden Ebenen herstellt.

› Ground floor Rez-de-chaussée Erdgeschoss

› First floor Premier étage Erstes Obergeschoss

› Section Section Schnitt

Direct sunlight is filtered into the dining-room area directly below through two glass panels in the floor.

La lumière directe du jour est filtrée vers la salle à manger en dessous par deux panneaux de verre dans le sol.

Durch die beiden Glasplatten im Fußboden fällt direktes Sonnenlicht in das darunter liegende Speisezimmer.

Canadian pine covers most of the floor, although there are traces of marble in the entrance, kitchen and bathroom.

La plupart des sols sont recouverts de pin canadien, bien que le marbre ponctue l'entrée, la cuisine et la salle de bains.

Der größte Teil des Bodens ist mit dem Holz der kanadischen Hemlocktanne belegt. Im Eingangsbereich, in der Küche und im Badezimmer ist der Bodenbelag teilweise aus Marmor.

Park Avenue Loft

Ayhan Ozan Architects
New York, United States

To construct this loft, the existing interior was gutted and the bare space was taken as the starting point for the renovation. Etched glass, the most important material present, was used to create divisions that optimize the circulation of light. The concept was developed around an open, sky-lit kitchen designed as a free-standing island within the living area to enhance the feeling of spaciousness. Furthermore, daylight was required to penetrate all the areas in the loft. To achieve this, no single wall reaches the ceiling, and a select few are surrounded by glass. The two large walls at either end of the living-room, framed from behind by the etched glass panels, mark the passageway into the private areas and act as an attractive backdrop for paintings and other objects. Closets were integrated into the perimeter windowsills to provide extra storage, and their wide surface also doubles as additional seating for social occasions.

Ce loft est le fruit de la rénovation d'un espace intérieur vide et dépouillé. Le recours au verre gravé à l'acide, matériau omniprésent dans ce projet, a permis de réaliser un système de partition optimalisant la circulation de la lumière. Le concept architectural a été développé autour d'un bloc cuisine ouvert et lumineux, posé tel un îlot au cœur de la salle de séjour, pour rehausser la sensation d'espace. En outre, toutes les zones du loft devant recevoir la lumière du jour, aucun mur ne touche le plafond et seuls quelques-uns uns sont gainés de verre. Deux murs situés à chaque extrémité du salon, encadrés à l'arrière par des panneaux en verre gravés à l'acide, marquent le passage vers les sphères privées et servent de support original pour tableaux ou autres objets. La superficie étendue du périmètre des rebords de fenêtres permet d'y intégrer des armoires offrant un supplément de rangement, et de doubler le nombre de places assises lors de réceptions.

Um dieses Loft zu bauen, wurde die existierende Struktur vollständig entkernt und als Ausgangspunkt für die Renovierung benutzt. Hauptsächlich wurde geätztes Glas eingesetzt, um Raumteiler zu schaffen, die Licht durchlassen. Der Mittelpunkt des Raums ist eine offene Küche mit Dachfenster, die eine freistehende Insel im Wohnbereich bildet und so das Gefühl von Weite noch verstärkt. Außerdem sollte Tageslicht in alle Winkel gelangen. Deshalb reicht keine Wand bis zur Decke, und einige der Wände sind von Glas umgeben. Die beiden großen Seitenwände des Wohnzimmers, die von hinten mit geätzten Glaspaneelen versehen sind, markieren den Übergang zu den privaten Räumen und bilden einen attraktiven Hintergrund für Gemälde und andere Objekte. In den Fensterbänken wurden Wandschränke untergebracht, um zusätzlichen Platz zu schaffen; darüber hinaus dienen die Fensterbänke auch als zusätzliche Sitzgelegenheit.

The concept was developed around an open, sky-lit kitchen designed as a free-standing island within the living area to enhance the feeling of spaciousness.

Le concept architectural évolue autour du bloc cuisine ouvert et lumineux, posé tel un îlot au cœur de la salle de séjour pour rehausser la sensation d'espace.

Ausgangspunkt des Konzeptes war die offene Küche mit Dachfenster, die wie eine freistehende Insel mitten im Wohnbereich liegt, was das Gefühl von Offenheit und Geräumigkeit noch verstärkt.

One of the main objectives of the design was to allow daylight to penetrate all the areas of the loft, thus brightening up the dark wood on the floors and in the kitchen.

L'idée essentielle qui anime le design est de laisser entrer la lumière dans toutes les zones du loft, éclaircissant ainsi le bois sombre des sols et de la cuisine.

Eines der Hauptziele dieses Projektes war es, das Tageslicht in alle Zonen des Lofts dringen zu lassen und so das dunkle Holz der Fußböden und der Küche heller wirken zu lassen.

› **Plan** Plan Grundriss

Glass Bridge

David Hotson
New York, United States

A complete renovation of these premises led to the creation of a generous, two-story space designed to adapt to a young couple with children. The main volume is delineated by full-height walls on three sides and carried across the fourth side by the glass and aluminum mezzanine railings and the overhanging upper-level bedroom. The kitchen and dining area, media room, and bridge are configured as secondary volumes sheathed in translucent glass. On the mezzanine level, the floor joining the media room to the children's bedrooms takes the form of a laminated-glass bridge passing over the dining area. To allow the private rooms to receive light and connect with the living space, the partitions separating them were fashioned from etched-glass panels framed in aluminum and made with hinged leaves. The materials are treated as the surfaces of concave spaces and volume is explored as an architectural space rather than a sculptural form.

Entièrement restauré, ce lieu s'est converti en un loft spacieux sur deux niveaux, pour un jeune couple avec enfants. Le volume principal, délimité par des murs tout en hauteur sur trois côtés, s'élance vers le quatrième côté grâce à la grille de verre et d'aluminium de la mezzanine et à la chambre suspendue du niveau supérieur. La cuisine et la salle à manger, la pièce réservée à la télévision et au bridge sont configurées comme des volumes annexes, gainés de verre translucide. Au niveau de la mezzanine, le sol reliant la salle de télévision aux chambres d'enfants, se transforme en passerelle de verre feuilleté, enjambant la salle à manger. Les cloisons, en panneaux de verre gravé encadrés d'aluminium, rendent les espaces privés plus lumineux et les relient à la pièce à vivre. Les matériaux sont traités comme des surfaces d'espaces concaves. Dans l'étude des volumes, l'architecture de l'espace prime sur la forme sculpturale.

Durch den Umbau dieses Gebäudes entstand ein großzügiger zweistöckiger Raum für ein junges Paar mit Kindern. Das Hauptvolumen wird auf drei Seiten von deckenhohen Wänden begrenzt, auf der vierten von dem Geländer des Zwischengeschosses aus Glas und Aluminium und dem hervorstehenden Schlafzimmer im oberen Stockwerk. Der Küchen- und Essbereich, das Medienzimmer und die Brücke bilden mit Glas verkleidete, sekundäre Volumen. Auf dem Zwischengeschoss wird der Flur, der das Medienzimmer mit dem Kinderzimmer verbindet, zu einer verkleideten Glasbrücke über das Esszimmer. Damit Tageslicht in die privaten Zimmer fällt und diese mit dem Wohnbereich verbunden bleiben, bestehen die Raumteiler aus geätzten Glasscheiben mit Aluminiumrahmen und Flügeln mit Scharnieren. Die Materialien werden wie Oberflächen konkaver Räume behandelt.

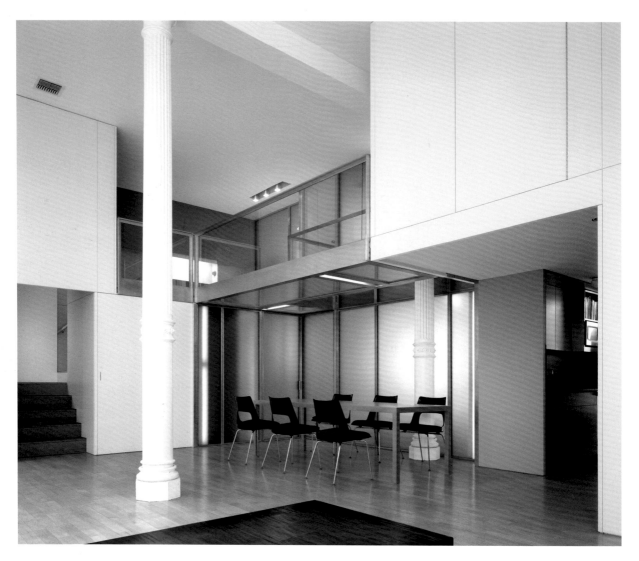

The white columns and the wooden flooring create a welcome contrast to the glass and aluminum railings on the mezzanine.

Les colonnes blanches et le sol boisé créent un beau contraste avec le verre et l'aluminium de la balustrade de la mezzanine.

Die weißen Säulen und der Holzfußboden schaffen einen willkommenen Kontrast zu den Glas- und Aluminiumschienen des Zwischengeschosses.

> **First floor** Premier étage Erstes Obergeschoss

> **Ground floor** Rez-de-chaussée Erdgeschoss

The floor that connects the media room to the children's bedrooms was constructed of laminated glass and configured as a bridge passing over the dining area.

Le sol, reliant la salle de télévision aux chambres d'enfants, se transforme en passerelle de verre feuilleté qui enjambe la salle à manger.

Der Fußboden im Medienraum und im Kinderschlafzimmer besteht aus beschichtetem Glas und bildet eine Brücke, die über den Essbereich führt.

Wall Street Loft

Chroma AD
New York, United States

In 1995, New York's City Hall encouraged contractors to convert empty office buildings in lower Manhattan into homes. The real estate group Time Equities took advantage of the proposal and hired the architectural team Chroma AD to remodel a six-story building into 13 lofts. The dramatic shadows and piercing rays of natural light found in this area are the conceptual inspiration for this project. By creating luminous white boxes and punctuating them with black elements, the architects hoped to reflect the feel of Wall Street. Wall-to-wall windows and enormous ceilings take advantage of all available daylight. Highly reflective epoxy-resin floors bounce light throughout the loft with the monolithic black kitchen. The removal of false ceilings allowed the concrete beams to be exposed for the first time. The kitchen, bathrooms, and open spaces were drawn up to harmonize with the existing beams and columns.

En 1995, le City Hall de New York a encouragé les constructeurs à convertir en logements les bureaux vides situés dans le bas Manhattan. Le groupe immobilier Time Equities a répondu à l'offre et a chargé le cabinet d'architectes Chroma AD de remodeler un immeuble de six étages en 13 lofts. La conception du projet s'est inspirée du jeu d'ombre et de lumière naturelle théâtral qui règne dans ce quartier. Par le biais de boîtes blanches lumineuses, ponctuées d'éléments noirs, les architectes ont cherché à reproduire l'ambiance de Wall Street. Les immenses fenêtres, dont sont dotées les hautes pièces, absorbent toute la lumière du jour possible. Des sols en résine époxy reflètent la lumière et la renvoient dans tout le loft, doté d'une cuisine monolithique noire. Le retrait des faux plafonds a permis de découvrir pour la première fois les poutres en béton. La cuisine, les salles de bains et les espaces de vie sont conçus pour s'intégrer harmonieusement aux poutres et colonnes préexistantes.

Im Jahr 1995 ermutigte die Stadtverwaltung von New York die Bauunternehmer dazu, Bürogebäude in Lower Manhattan in Wohnungen umzugestalten. Die Immobiliengruppe Time Equities nutzte dieses Angebot aus und nahm das Architektenteam Chroma AD unter Vertrag, um ein sechsstöckiges Gebäude in 13 Lofts umzubauen. Das Spiel aus Schatten und grellem Licht in diesem Bezirk diente den Planern als konzeptuelle Inspiration. Sie gestalteten helle, weiße Kästen mit gezielt eingesetzten, schwarzen Elementen, um so die Atmosphäre der Wall Street zu reflektieren. Durch die Wände einnehmenden Fenster und hohen Decken dringt reichlich Tageslicht. Reflektierende, mit Epoxidharz beschichtete Böden lassen das Licht durch das Loft bis zur schwarzen Küche vordringen. Die abgehängten Decken wurden entfernt und die Betonbalken sichtbar gemacht. Die Küche vordringen, das Bad und die offenen Räume harmonieren mit den alten Balken und Säulen.

The wall-to-ceiling windows bath the dining room with light during the day, while highly reflective epoxy-resin floors bounce light throughout the loft.

Les baies vitrées baignent la pièce de lumière naturelle pendant la journée, renvoyée par les sols en résine époxy dans tout le loft.

Tagsüber fällt durch die bis zur Decke reichenden Fenster sehr viel Licht, das mithilfe der reflektierenden, mit Epoxidharz beschichteten Fußböden in das gesamte Loft vordringt.

› Plan Plan Grundriss

By creating bright, white boxes and punctuating them with black elements, the architects hoped to reflect the feel of Wall Street.

En créant de larges boîtes blanches, émaillées d'éléments noirs, l'architecte a tenté de recréer l'ambiance de Wall Street.

Der Architekt gestaltete helle, weiße Kästen mit gezielt eingesetzten, schwarzen Elementen, um die Atmosphäre der Wall Street zu reflektieren.

Carlo Berarducci
Rome, Italy

Transformable Loft

This loft, located in Rome, Italy, consists of two areas: a large rectangular space flanked by a wall of windows and another with glass doors that open onto a private terrace. The areas are divided by a sequence of pillars and panels. Two large sliding panels screen off the living and dining areas from the entrance, while a set of hinged panels fold out to close off one area so that it can be used as a guest bedroom. These folding panels reduce to the width of the pillar, leaving the living space completely open. A suspended blue wall and a stone platform into which the mattress is inserted delineate the bedroom. In the kitchen, the black granite countertop extends beyond the kitchen module to serve as a bar or breakfast table. In the bathroom, the same intense blue used as a backdrop to the bedroom covers the floors.

Ce loft, situé à Rome, en Italie, offre deux espaces : l'un est un large rectangle flanqué d'un mur de fenêtres et l'autre est doté de portes en verre qui s'ouvrent sur une terrasse privée. Une série de colonnes et de panneaux scandent l'espace. Deux cloisons coulissantes séparent le salon et la salle à manger de l'entrée et une série de partitions se déplient pour clore l'espace et créer une chambre d'amis. Ces panneaux réduits à la taille d'une colonne, créent un espace de vie totalement ouvert. Un mur bleu suspendu et une plate-forme en pierre dotée d'un matelas intégré définissent la chambre à coucher. Dans la cuisine, le plan de travail en granit noir prolonge le module de la cuisine et sert de bar ou de table pour le petit déjeuner. Le sol de la salle de bains est revêtu du même bleu intense utilisé en toile de fond pour la chambre.

Dieses Loft in Rom besteht aus zwei Bereichen: einem großen, rechteckigen Raum begrenzt durch eine Fensterwand und einem anderen mit Glastüren, die zur privaten Terrasse führen. Die verschiedenen Bereiche sind durch Pfeiler und Wandelemente unterteilt. Zwei große Gleitpaneele schirmen den Wohn- und Essbereich vom Eingang ab, während eine Reihe von gefalteten Paneelen auseinandergezogen werden können, um ein Gästezimmer abzuteilen. Diese faltbaren Paneele reduzieren die Breite des Pfeilers und lassen den Wohnbereich völlig offen. Eine hängende, blaue Wand und eine Steinplattform, in der die Matratze eingelassen ist, begrenzen das Schlafzimmer. In der Küche geht die Arbeitsfläche aus schwarzem Granit über das Küchenmodul hinaus und dient als Bar und Frühstückstisch. Im Badezimmer findet man das gleiche intensive Blau des Schlafzimmers im Fußboden.

The parquet floor, white walls, and soft colors of the furniture create a warm atmosphere throughout the living-room.

Le parquet, les murs blancs et les couleurs douces des meubles, imprègnent tout le salon d'une atmosphère chaude.

Durch den Parkettboden, die weißen Wände und die Möbel in sanften Farben herrscht im ganzen Wohnzimmer eine warme Atmosphäre.

› **Plan** Plan Grundriss

The black granite countertop extends beyond the kitchen module to serve as a bar or breakfast table.

Le plan de travail, en granit noir, prolonge le module de la cuisine et sert de bar ou de table pour le petit déjeuner.

Die Arbeitsfläche aus schwarzem Granit reicht über das Küchenmodul hinaus und dient so auch als Bar oder Frühstückstisch.

The floor in the bathroom displays the same bright blue color that is used as a backdrop for the bedroom.

Le sol de la salle de bains est revêtu du même bleu intense utilisé en toile de fond pour la chambre.

Der Boden im Badezimmer ist im gleichen Hellblau gehalten, das auch als Hintergrundfarbe für das Schlafzimmer dient.

Attic in Vienna

The main concerns in residential architecture are functional or aesthetic, but Lichtblau & Wagner have also introduced energy-saving concepts into this field. To achieve greater efficiency, these young Austrian architects have ruled out superficial luxuries like marble bathrooms, pointless terraces, and grandiose entrances to concentrate on a flexible project that economizes on energy, expense, and space. Four basic, 538-sq. ft. units were conceived. They are organized in pairs, with an additional space that may be added to one apartment or the other. This alteration is easy to achieve by simply relocating partitions. The communal spaces contain a storeroom, a laundry, and a multipurpose area for meetings or parties (offsetting the lack of space in the studios). Positions have been suggested for the kitchen and bathroom but they can be moved without any building work. The clients can rearrange their home according to their tastes or requirements.

L'architecture d'habitation a pour principes essentiels, le fonctionnel ou l'esthétique. Mais Lichtblau & Wagner y a ajouté le concept d'économie d'énergie. Pour plus d'efficacité, ces jeunes architectes autrichiens ont éliminé le luxe superficiel, comme les salles de bains en marbre, les terrasses inutiles et les halls d'entrée grandioses pour se consacrer à des projets modulables, offrant un gain d'énergie, de coût et d'espace. Ils ont conçu quatre unités de base de 50 m², organisées par paire et dotées d'un espace supplémentaire que l'on peut ajouter à un appartement ou à un autre. Ces modifications sont facilitées par des cloisons modulables. L'espace commun abrite un coin rangement, une buanderie et une zone polyvalente pour les réunions ou les fêtes (compensant le manque d'espace dans les studios). Les emplacements pour la cuisine et les salles de bains sont prévus mais sont modifiables. Les clients peuvent réaménager leur intérieur selon leurs besoins.

In der Wohnungsarchitektur wird meist der Schwerpunkt auf Funktionalität und Ästhetik gelegt. Lichtblau & Wagner legen ebenso großen Wert auf energiesparendes Bauen. Dazu verzichten diese jungen österreichischen Architekten auf oberflächlichen Luxus wie Marmorbadezimmer, unnütze Terrassen und grandiose Eingangsbereiche und konzentrieren sich auf eine flexible Planung, bei der Energie, Kosten und Raum eingespart werden. Es wurden vier 50 m² große Basiseinheiten entworfen, paarweise organisiert. Ein zusätzlicher Raum kann sehr einfach einer der beiden Wohnungen hinzugefügt werden, indem die Raumteiler umplatziert werden. Es gibt einen gemeinsamen Lagerraum, einen Wäscheraum und einen Vielzweckbereich, in dem gefeiert werden kann (um den Platzmangel auszugleichen). Die Lage der Küchen und Badezimmer können verändert und somit das Haus individuell gestaltet werden.

The space beneath the sliding windows may be used as a terrace, gallery, or greenhouse. Drapes separate this space from the rest of the home, creating a sensation of warmth and comfort.

L'espace en dessous des baies vitrées coulissantes peut servir de terrasse, de galerie ou de serre. Il est séparé du reste de la maison par des tentures, créant une sensation de chaleur et de confort.

Der Raum unterhalb der Schiebefenster kann als Terrasse, Galerie oder Wintergarten benutzt werden. Dieser Raum ist durch Vorhänge vom Rest des Hauses abgetrennt. Er wirkt warm und komfortabel.

› Plan Plan Grundriss

Loft on Rue Popincourt

Gaëlle Hamonic and
Jean-Christophe Masson
Paris, France

This loft, in which an old structure coexists with a modern architectural approach, was configured as a space in which natural light is omnipresent. This project, a radical intervention in a practically empty space, was based on two premises: on the one hand, the preservation of the façades and the roofs and, on the other, a new construction in the center of the home, once occupied by the coach house. The architect took advantage not only of the existing structure but also the back patio, now a garden, which provides all the bedrooms with light and a sense of spaciousness. Furthermore, the respect for the design of the original façade allows the building to blend in with the neighboring buildings. The lobby leads to the sitting room, which is a large space flooded with light that gives on to the patio. The filters of light are a line of bamboo in the patio and screens made of translucent polycarbonate.

Ce loft où l'ancienne structure côtoie une approche architecturale moderne, a été conçu comme un espace où la lumière naturelle est omniprésente. Ce projet couvre la restauration totale d'un espace pratiquement vide et comporte deux idées directrices : d'une part, préserver les façades et les toitures et d'autre part, construire un nouvel espace au centre de l'habitation, ancienne maison de cocher. L'architecte a su tirer parti de la structure préexistante et aussi du patio à l'arrière du bâtiment, transformé en jardin, dotant toutes les chambres de lumière naturelle et d'une sensation d'espace. En outre, grâce au maintien du design de la façade d'origine, le bâtiment se fond avec les autres édifices environnants. La réception mène au salon, un espace généreux inondé de lumière qui s'ouvre sur le patio où une rangée de bambous et de paravents en polycarbonate translucide filtrent la lumière.

Dieses Loft, in dem die alte Struktur mit modernen Elemente kombiniert ist, wurde als ein Raum geplant, in dem es überall Tageslicht gibt. Der Entwurf, bei dem ein radikaler Eingriff in einen praktisch leeren Raum vorgenommen wurde, ging von zwei Voraussetzungen aus. Einerseits mussten die Fassaden und das Dach erhalten bleiben, andererseits wurde ein Neubau im Zentrum des Hauses, wo sich einst der Wagenschuppen befand, durchgeführt. Der Architekt nutzte nicht nur die bereits vorhandene Struktur, sondern auch den Hinterhof, der heute ein Garten ist, um Licht in alle Räume zu bringen und ein Gefühl von Weite zu schaffen. Da die Originalfassade erhalten blieb, fügt sich das Gebäude harmonisch in die Umgebung ein. Der Korridor führt zum Wohnzimmer, ein großer, lichtdurchströmter Raum zum Hof. Eine Bambusreihe im Innenhof und Schirme aus lichtdurchlässigem Polycarbonat filtern das Tageslicht.

› Section Section Schnitt

› First floor Premier étage Erstes Obergeschoss

› Ground floor Rez-de-chaussée Erdgeschoss

Potter Loft

Resolution: 4 Architecture
New York, United States

The refurbishment of this loft in New York's Chelsea district reflects the client's simple lifestyle. The layout is governed by the concept of open space, moving from the centrally located kitchen to the bathrooms and bedrooms at the back of the apartment. The kitchen area is surrounded by different types of surfaces that define the thresholds of the space. Concrete panels mark off the living room. Banks of lights on the dining-room ceiling, including a distinctive overhead wedge-shape lamp, provide intense illumination. The building's security entrance consists of a sliding door built with a custom-made metal sheet. A pivoting door provides the bedroom with more intimacy and allows light to enter as it is opened more fully. The windows to the street provide views of the exterior, although privacy is protected by Venetian blinds, which also control the flow of light.

La rénovation de ce loft situé dans le quartier de Chelsea à New York reflète la simplicité du style de vie du client. La conception s'articule autour d'un espace ouvert qui, partant de la cuisine située au centre, mène aux salles de bains et aux chambres à coucher à l'arrière de l'appartement. L'aire de la cuisine est entourée de différents types de revêtements qui définissent le seuil des autres espaces. Des panneaux de béton délimitent le salon. Des sources de lumière au plafond du salon, y compris une lampe spéciale angulaire, suspendue, dispensent un éclairage intense. L'entrée surveillée de l'édifice est dotée d'une porte coulissante en feuille de métal construite sur commande. Une porte pivotante confère plus d'intimité à la chambre et de par son ouverture, permet à la lumière d'entrer. Les fenêtres sur la rue ont vue sur l'extérieur et sont dotées de stores à l'italienne pour préserver l'intimité et contrôler le flux de lumière.

Die Sanierung dieses Lofts im New Yorker Distrikt Chelsea spiegelt den einfachen Lebensstil des Kunden wider. Wichtig ist das Konzept des offenen Raumes, das die Küche im Zentrum, die Badezimmer und die Schlafzimmer hinten in der Wohnung umfasst. Der Küchenbereich ist von unterschiedlichen Oberflächen umgeben, die die Grenzen des Raums definieren. Betonplatten markieren den Wohnbereich. Lichtbalken in der Esszimmerdecke und eine besondere, keilförmige Lampe sorgen für intensive Beleuchtung. Der Sicherheitseingang des Gebäudes besteht aus einer Schiebetür aus maßgefertigten Metallplatten. Eine schwenkbare Tür trennt das Schlafzimmer ab und lässt viel Licht herein, wenn sie ganz geöffnet ist. Durch das Fenster zur Straße hat man einen guten Ausblick, der Blick nach innen wird jedoch durch Jalousien begrenzt, die auch den Lichteinfall regulieren.

The kitchen and dining area share a common, open space, facilitating conversation between those who are cooking and their guests.

La cuisine et la salle à manger se partagent l'espace ouvert, facilitant la conversation entre le cuisinier et ses invités.

Die Küche und der Essbereich liegen in einem gemeinsamen, sehr offenen Raum, sodass die Gastgeber sich beim Kochen mit ihren Gästen unterhalten können.

› **Plan** Plan Grundriss

The architect's aim was to keep the structure intact by introducing new floors to hold up the rooms without removing any of the existing brick walls.

L'architecte voulait garder la structure d'origine intacte en intégrant de nouveaux sols pour rénover les pièces, sans ôter aucun des murs de briques existants.

Ziel des Architekten war es, die ursprüngliche Struktur zu erhalten. Er zog neue Böden ein, die die Räume stützen, ohne dabei die existierenden Ziegelwände entfernen zu müssen.

Refurbishment of an Attic

Marco Savorelli
Milan, Italy

In this project, located in the historic center of Milan, the architect disregarded the space's former layout and focused on a new distribution plan. The general concept was to integrate all the rooms into a single space, avoiding doors and interior partitions. The choice of only one type of flooring, dark wood, contributes to a feeling of unity while contrasting with the clean, white walls. The architect used the sloping ceilings to create a main axis of circulation in the center of the dwelling at the highest point. The spaces for activities related to leisure and relaxation were constructed on the perimeter. The service areas (bathroom, kitchen, and toilets) are monolithic volumes. Since this loft is a succession of spaces with no defined frontiers, the entry becomes the living-room, and the bedroom melts into the bathroom.

Dans ce projet, situé dans le centre historique de Milan, l'architecte n'a pas tenu compte de l'ancienne planification et s'est concentré sur un nouveau schéma. L'idée générale est d'intégrer toutes les pièces en un espace unique, éliminant portes et cloisons intérieures. Le choix d'un seul type de sol – en bois sombre – accentue la sensation d'unité et contraste avec la pureté des murs blancs. L'architecte a tiré parti des plafonds inclinés pour créer un grand axe de passage au cœur de l'habitation, en son point culminant. Les espaces consacrés aux loisirs et à la détente sont construits sur le pourtour. Les aires de services – salle de bains, cuisine et toilettes – sont des volumes monolithiques. Ce loft étant une succession d'espaces sans délimitations définies, l'entrée se métamorphose en salon et la chambre à coucher fusionne avec la salle de bains.

Bei diesem Projekt im historischen Stadtkern von Mailand veränderte der Architekt die ursprüngliche Raumaufteilung vollständig. Das Allgemeinkonzept war es, alle Funktionen in einem einzigen Raum unterzubringen und Türen und innere Raumteiler zu vermeiden. Der durchgehend aus dunklem Holz gefertigte Fußbodenbelag trägt zu diesem Gefühl von Einheit bei und steht im Gegensatz zu den glatten weißen Wänden. Der Architekt benutzte die geneigten Decken, um eine Hauptachse für den Durchgang in der Mitte der Wohnung unter dem höchsten Punkt der Decke zu schaffen. Die Raumabschnitte für Freizeit und Entspannung liegen am Rand. Die funktionellen Räume wie Badezimmer, Küche und Toiletten sind monolithische Volumen. Da dieses Loft aus einer Abfolge von Räumen ohne definierte Grenzen besteht, wird aus dem Eingangsbereich das Wohnzimmer, und das Schlafzimmer verschmilzt mit dem Badezimmer.

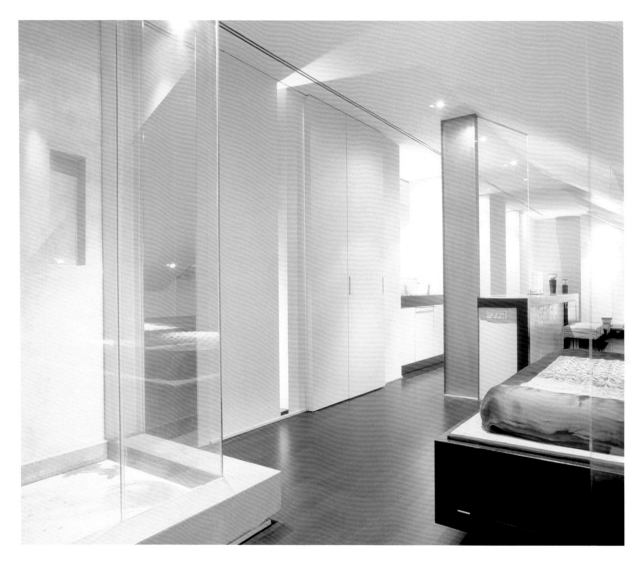

The shower, made of glass, is located in the bedroom and appears as an independent volume that is visually connected to the rest of the room.

La douche en verre forme dans la chambre à coucher un bloc indépendant relié visuellement au reste de la pièce.

Die gläserne Duschkabine befindet sich im Schlafzimmer und wirkt wie ein unabhängiges Volumen, das visuell mit dem Rest des Raumes in Verbindung steht.

› **Plan** Plan Grundriss

Two Lofts on Passage Gauthier

Frédéric Jung and
Claudine Dreyfus
Paris, France

The architects Frédéric Jung and Claudine Dreyfus refurbished this industrial building to make room for two self-contained residences that are only connected by a communal terrace on the upper floor. Both units had to be independent of each other, so the architects divided the building with a vertical wall and added another level. The conversion focused its attention more on the construction and design than the details, reflecting the building's location and the precision of the architectural project. The interior program developed an extremely dynamic vertical concept, in a sequence centered on the helical staircases in each loft. The same principle was applied in both spaces, involving a large living room and several blocks that make up the bedrooms, the bathrooms and the closets. The terrace, with a floor of wooden planks, gazes out over the streets of Paris.

Les architectes Frédéric Jung et Claudine Dreyfus ont restauré ce bâtiment industriel pour y installer deux résidences mitoyennes qui partagent une terrasse commune à l'étage supérieur, trait d'union entre les deux. Les deux unités devant être indépendantes l'une de l'autre, les architectes ont divisé le bâtiment par un mur vertical et ont ajouté un deuxième niveau. Ce projet de restauration, davantage axé sur la construction et le design que sur les détails, reflète la situation du bâtiment et la précision de la conception architecturale. Le concept intérieur développe une dynamique verticale extrême autour de l'axe représenté par l'escalier hélicoïdal de chaque loft. Les deux habitations sont régies par le même principe de base, à savoir un grand salon et une série de blocs pour les chambres, les salles de bains et les toilettes. De la terrasse, en lattes de bois, la vue s'étend sur les rues de Paris.

Die Architekten Frédéric Jung und Claudine Dreyfus sanierten dieses Industriegebäude, um zwei unabhängige Wohnungen zu schaffen, die durch eine Terrasse im Obergeschoss verbunden sind. Beide Einheiten sollten unabhängig sein, deshalb unterteilten die Architekten das Gebäude mit einer vertikalen Wand und fügten eine weitere Ebene hinzu. Bei der Gestaltung der Wohnungen wurde das Augenmerk mehr auf die Konstruktion und das Design als auf die Einzelheiten gerichtet. Dadurch werden der Standort des Gebäudes und die Präzision der architektonischen Planung reflektiert. Die Raumgestaltung basiert auf einem dynamischen, vertikalen Konzept, eine Sequenz, die auf der spiralförmigen Treppe in jedem Loft beruht. In beiden Einheiten folgt die Raumgestaltung dem Prinzip, ein großes Wohnzimmer mit verschiedenen Blöcken für Badezimmer und Wandschränke zu formen. Die mit Holzplanken belegte Terrasse bietet eine schöne Aussicht auf die Straßen von Paris.

Although the street façade remains practically unchanged, two panels of glass bricks have been put into the rear to allow sunlight to penetrate inside.

La façade reste pratiquement inchangée à l'exception de deux cloisons de pavés de verre installées à l'arrière du bâtiment pour permettre à la lumière de pénétrer l'intérieur.

Die Fassade zur Straße hin blieb fast unverändert, während man an der Hinterfassade zwei Platten aus Glasbausteinen einsetzte, damit Tageslicht in die Räume fallen kann.

› Ground floor Rez-de-chaussée Erdgeschoss   › First floor Premier étage Erstes Obergeschoss   › Second floor Deuxième étage Zweite Obergeschoss

The interior program developed an extremely dynamic vertical concept, involving a large, open living room.

L'intérieur, conçu selon un concept général de verticalité, dispose d'un salon large et ouvert.

Die Innengestaltung erfolgte nach einem sehr dynamischen, vertikalen Konzept, zu dem ein großes, offenes Wohnzimmer gehörte.

Baron Loft

Deborah Berke
New York, United States

The architect Deborah Berke focused on perfecting and reducing the elements to achieve a pure and elegant minimalist style in this renovation for an art director and his family. The materials used include smooth plaster on the walls, while the flooring is of ebonized oak. Polished schist blocks where used in the bathroom, next to oiled walnut slabs, brushed stainless steel splashes, white glass, and white window scrims. Each of these materials has the least detail possible. Much of the furniture is built into the house and displays the owner's extensive art collection. A strict color palette gives way to a sober design sprinkled with subtle doses of warm tones. The kitchen is hidden behind walnut doors, while a translucent glass wall conceals the master bedroom.

Dans ce projet de rénovation pour un directeur artistique et sa famille, l'architecte Deborah Berke a misé sur la perfection et la réduction des éléments pour obtenir un style minimaliste épuré tout en élégance. Les matériaux se déclinent en plâtres lisses pour les murs. Les sols sont en chêne aux allures d'ébène. Des dalles d'ardoise polie ont été posées dans la salle de bains, en alternance avec des lattes de noyer huilé, des touches d'acier inoxydable brossé, du verre blanc comme les châssis de fenêtre. Chacun de ces matériaux est dépourvu de motifs. L'importante collection d'œuvre d'art du propriétaire est exposée sur les meubles intégrés à l'architecture de la maison. Un nuancier de couleurs sobres met en valeur un design aux lignes épurées, ponctuées des touches subtiles de teintes chaudes. La cuisine se cache derrière des murs en noyer et une paroi de verre translucide dissimule la chambre des maîtres.

Die Architektin Deborah Berke konzentrierte sich auf eine Perfektion und Reduktion von Elementen, um beim Ausbau dieses Lofts für einen Art Director und seine Familie einen reinen, eleganten und minimalistischen Stil zu erzielen. Die Wände sind glatt verputzt, die Fußböden mit gebeizter Eiche belegt. Die im Badezimmer verwendeten Materialien sind polierte Schieferblöcke, Tafeln aus geöltem Nussbaum, ein Spritzschutz aus gebürstetem Edelstahl, Milchglas und weiße Leinengardinen. All diese Materialien sind so einfach wie möglich gehalten. Viele Möbel sind eingebaut und dienen als Ausstellungsflächen für die umfassende Kunstsammlung des Eigentümers. Eine strenge Farbpalette lässt die Gestaltung sehr schlicht wirken, vereinzelt werden gezielt warme Töne eingesetzt. Die Küchentüren sind aus Nussbaum und das Hauptschlafzimmer befindet sich hinter einer lichtdurchlässigen Glaswand.

The lighting, red furniture, and ebonized oak floors add color and so set up a contrast with the plain white walls.

L'éclairage, le mobilier rouge et les sols en chêne couleur ébène ajoutent une note de couleur qui contraste avec la blancheur des murs.

Die leuchtend roten Möbel und die schwarz gebeizten Eichenböden setzen Farbakzente und dienen als Kontrast zu den schlichten, weißen Wänden.

› **Plan** Plan Grundriss

Some of the furniture is built into the house and display the owner's extensive art collection.

Une partie du mobilier est intégrée à la maison et permet au maître des lieux d'exposer son importante collection d'objets d'art.

Einige der Möbel sind eingebaut und dienen als Ausstellungsflächen für die umfassende Kunstsammlung des Eigentümers.

Philippe Demougeot
Paris, France

Loft Paris 10ème

A façade of glass bricks, a vestige of the paint and wallpaper store that once occupied the premises, conceals a large space on the ground floor and basement that was converted into a warm, light-filled loft residence. In order for the light to penetrate everywhere the conversion removed part of the ceilings that separated the floors in the entrance and in the rear. Glass bricks were also used in the inner walls, blurring the view so that light can reach the bedrooms without any loss of privacy. The ground floor was designed to achieve a warm, cozy atmosphere for the bedrooms and the office, while the basement is a large space containing the communal areas. The axis of the home is a glass and stainless steel staircase that adds to the interplay of light; it goes right into the kitchen, where it even serves as a table.

La façade de briques de verre – vestige du magasin de papiers peints situé sur ce site – abrite un rez-de-chaussée et un sous-sol, immense espace converti en un loft chaleureux et inondé de lumière naturelle. Une partie des plafonds séparant les espaces a été supprimée à l'entrée et à l'arrière, pour laisser pénétrer un maximum de lumière. Les murs intérieurs, également en briques de verre translucides, mais non transparentes, permettent à la lumière de pénétrer dans les chambres tout en préservant l'intimité. Le design du rez-de-chaussée crée une atmosphère douillette et chaude dans les chambres et le bureau. Le sous-sol, très spacieux, abrite les parties communes. L'escalier de verre et d'acier inoxydable est l'axe de l'appartement dont il accentue le jeu de lumière. Il s'inscrit au cœur de la cuisine où il se métamorphose en table.

Eine Fassade aus Glasziegeln, die noch aus dem ehemaligen Farb- und Tapetengeschäft stammt, das sich einst hier befand, verbirgt große Räume im Erd- und Kellergeschoss, die zu einer warmen und hellen Wohnung umgebaut wurden. Damit das Tageslicht überall hingelangen konnte, wurden Teile der Decke entfernt, die die Stockwerke am Eingang und im hinteren Teil trennten. Ebenso wurden Glasbausteine für die Innenwände verwendet, die Licht durchlassen, aber die Privatsphäre schützen. Die Atmosphäre im Erdgeschoss, wo sich die Schlafzimmer und das Büro befinden, ist sehr freundlich, das Kellergeschoss ist ein weiter, offener, gemeinschaftlich nutzbarer Raum. Die Verbindungsachse dieser Wohnung ist die Treppe aus Glas und Edelstahl, die das Spiel mit dem Licht noch unterstreicht. Sie führt bis in die Küche, wo sie sogar als Tisch dient.

The home revolves around a glass and stainless-steel staircase that adds to the interplay of light characteristic of the entire space.

La maison évolue autour d'un escalier d'acier et de verre qui accentue le jeu de lumière, point d'orgue de l'espace entier.

Das Loft ist um eine Treppe aus Glas und Edelstahl angelegt, was das Spiel mit dem Licht, das den Raum prägt, noch unterstreicht.

› **Ground floor** Rez-de-chaussée Erdgeschoss

› **Basement** Sous-sol Kellergeschoss

The ground floor was designed to achieve a warm, cozy atmosphere for the bedrooms and the office, while the basement is a large, open space.

Le rez-de-chaussée est conçu pour créer une atmosphère chaleureuse et agréable dans les chambres et le bureau alors que le sous-sol est un espace généreux et ouvert.

Die Atmosphäre im Erdgeschoss, wo sich die Schlafzimmer und das Büro befinden, ist sehr warm und einladend. Das Kellergeschoss ist ein weiter, offener Raum.

Orange and White

Pablo Chiappori
Buenos Aires, Argentina

Based on simple lines combined with the use of noble materials, this project features a dynamic space in which each area possesses it own characteristic. Dark woods, natural stone, steel, and translucent fabrics in different textures are the most prominent materials, while neutral colors with different intensities create a soothing environment. The kitchen is concealed within a module alongside the entrance hall and incorporates a breakfast area with stools. The lounge, comfortably furnished and decorated in bright orange and white, leads to the upper level, which contains the bedroom suite. The views between the various spaces are filtered by dividing elements, such as the large, sliding wooden door that constitutes one of the home's main decorative features and disappears into the wall to reveal the bedroom. An en-suite bathroom reveals an open washing area and a more private shower and toilet.

Ce projet, qui allie lignes épurées et matériaux nobles, met en scène un espace dynamique où chaque zone a ses propres caractéristiques. Bois foncés, pierre naturelle, acier et voiles transparents de textures différentes sont les principaux matériaux qui régissent cette atmosphère calme, créée par un dégradé de couleurs claires plus ou moins intenses. Le long de l'entrée, un module abrite la cuisine et un coin repas doté de tabourets. Le séjour, aux meubles confortables et au décor dans les tons d'orange et de blanc soutenus, mène à l'étage où se trouve la grande chambre à coucher. Des éléments de séparation, comme de grandes portes coulissantes de bois, préservent l'intimité des divers espaces, mais peuvent coulisser dans le mur pour faire apparaître par exemple la chambre à coucher. Une salle de bains s'ouvre, à la manière d'une suite, sur une salle d'eau puis sur une sphère plus intime avec douche et toilettes.

Die Gestalter schufen einfache Linien in Kombination mit edlen Materialien. So entstanden dynamische Räume, in denen jeder Bereich seinen eigenen Charakter hat. Dunkles Holz, Naturstein, Stahl und lichtdurchlässige Gewebe in verschiedenen Texturen sind die hauptsächlich verwendeten Materialien. Neutrale Farben in unterschiedlicher Intensität schaffen eine beruhigende Umgebung. Die Küche ist hinter einem Modul verborgen, das am Eingangskorridor entlang verläuft und den Frühstücksbereich mit Stühlen aufnimmt. Das in Hellorange und Weiß dekorierte Wohnzimmer führt auf die obere Ebene, wo sich das große Schlafzimmer befindet. Durch Trennelemente wird dort die Intimsphäre gewahrt. Eins davon ist die Schiebetür aus Holz, die ganz in der Wand verschwinden kann, um das Schlafzimmer offen zu lassen. Daneben befindet sich ein Badezimmer mit einem offenen Waschbereich und einer geschlossenen Zone für Dusche und Toilette.

Comprising comfortable furniture and bright shades of white and orange, the living area leads to the upper level, which contains the bedroom suite.

Doté de meubles confortables et de tons soutenus blancs et orange, le salon mène à l'étage supérieur où se trouve la chambre à coucher qui ressemble à une suite.

Der Wohnbereich ist mit bequemen Möbeln und in hellen Weiß- und Orangetönen dekoriert und führt in die obere Ebene, in der sich das große Schlafzimmer befindet.

The interaction between the proportions of the horizontal spaces and the vertical voids, as well as the amount of natural light, serve to mark out the various areas in the loft.

L'interaction entre les espaces horizontaux et les vides verticaux, ainsi que le volume de la lumière naturelle, permettent de délimiter les espaces du loft.

Durch die Wechselwirkungen der horizontalen Räume mit den vertikalen Hohlräumen, sowie durch das einströmende Tageslicht werden die verschiedenen Bereiche in diesem Loft gekennzeichnet.

The kitchen is concealed within a module alongside the entrance hallway and incorporates a breakfast area with stools.

Le long du hall d'entrée, un module abrite la cuisine et un coin repas doté de tabourets.

Die Küche ist hinter einem Modul verborgen, das am Eingangskorridor entlang verläuft. Hier gibt es eine Frühstücksecke mit Stühlen.

White walls and neutral colors of different intensities create a soothing setting environment in which special elements stand out.

Murs blancs et couleurs neutres, d'intensités différentes, créent un environnement apaisant où certains éléments sont mis en valeur.

Weiße Wände und neutrale Farben verschiedener Intensität schaffen eine ruhige Wohnatmosphäre, in der einzelne Elemente auffallen.

In the bedroom, a window behind the bed looks onto the lower level, and an en-suite bathroom reveals an open wash area and a more private shower and toilet.

Dans la chambre à coucher, une fenêtre derrière le lit permet de voir le niveau inférieur. La salle de bains, en forme de suite, révèle une salle d'eau ouverte et une sphère plus intime avec douche et toilettes.

Im Schlafzimmer kann man von einem Fenster hinter dem Bett aus in die untere Ebene schauen. Das Badezimmer, das im gleichen Raum untergebracht ist, hat einen offenen Waschbereich und eine abgetrennte Zone für Dusche und Toilette.

Loft in London

Child Graddon Lewis
London, United Kingdom

The firm of Child Graddon Lewis converted this charming Victorian building in the heart of Covent Garden into loft-style apartments. They created 22 shells in the building, originally designed as a warehouse. The apartments are distributed over six stories, with a retail space on the ground floor. Flexibility lies at the heart of the design concept, which gives clients the freedom to create their own interior layout and develop their own truly unique space. The company designed the kitchen, the bathroom and some pieces of furniture, which were put at the disposal of the new owners. Carefully chosen additions like large sliding doors lead to balconies and terraces constructed with cedar flooring. New metal-framed windows and glass panels take advantage of the natural light entering the apartments. Outside, the designers adapted the historic building to create a stunning rear elevation that capitalizes on period details.

L'entreprise Child Graddon Lewis a réhabilité ce charmant édifice victorien, au cœur de Covent Garden, en des logements de style loft. Ils ont créé 22 modules, destinés à l'origine pour un entrepôt. Les appartements sont répartis sur six étages, le rez-de-chaussée étant réservé à un espace commercial. La flexibilité s'inscrit au cœur du concept design, permettant ainsi au client de moduler l'espace intérieur à sa guise pour créer un univers personnel et unique. La compagnie a conçu la cuisine, la salle de bains et certains meubles, mis à la disposition des nouveaux propriétaires ainsi que des éléments supplémentaires, bien choisis : portes coulissantes sur balcons et terrasses en bois de cèdre. Fenêtres à châssis de métal et cloisons de verre favorisent l'entrée de la lumière naturelle dans les appartements. À l'extérieur, les designers ont rehaussé à merveille la façade de l'édifice historique mettant en relief les détails d'époque.

Das Unternehmen Child Graddon Lewis baute dieses viktorianische Gebäude in Covent Garden in eine Reihe von Lofts um. Sie schufen 22 Einheiten in dem Gebäude, das einst als Lagerhaus diente. Die Appartements liegen auf sechs Stockwerken, im Erdgeschoss befindet sich ein Geschäft. Grundlage des Konzeptes war die Vielseitigkeit, die Möglichkeit für die Kunden, die Räume individuell und einzigartig zu gestalten. Das Unternehmen entwarf die Küche, das Badezimmer und ein paar Möbelstücke, die den neuen Besitzern zur Verfügung gestellt wurden. Zusätzliche Elemente wurden sorgfältig ausgewählt, wie zum Beispiel die Schiebetüren zu den Balkonen und Terrassen mit Böden aus Zedernholz. Neue Fenster mit Metallrahmen und Glasplatten lassen das Tageslicht in die Appartements dringen. Auch von außen veränderten die Architekten das historische Gebäude, indem sie eine verblüffende Erhebung bauten, um die historischen Elemente zu betonen.

The sink and floors are made of wood and the walls are clad with stone. The kitchen is a very practical and comfortable part of the house.

L'évier et les sols sont en bois et les murs sont habillés de pierre. La cuisine est un endroit de la maison où pratique et confort vont de paire.

Der Waschtisch und die Fußböden bestehen aus Holz, und die Wände sind mit Stein verkleidet. Die Küche ist sehr praktisch und komfortabel.

› Plans   Plans   Grundrisse

Nile Street Loft

McDowell & Benedetti
London, United Kingdom

This apartment is located on the top floor and roof level of a nineteenth-century warehouse in London. The façades were left untreated and the existing brickwork and floor slabs were exposed, while new service areas were located near the front door. The client's brief called for a one-bedroom apartment with home office space and a multi-purpose room that can be closed off and used as a second bedroom. The layout maximizes the sense of space by moving the original front door and creating a double-height entrance hall that visually connects the two floor levels and contains all the circulation areas. A skylight runs the full length of the top floor over this area, spreading natural light deep inside. The several large sliding and pivoting firedoors are hidden from view, ensuring a fluid relationship with the open-plan living/dining/kitchen areas while fulfilling their function in the case of a fire.

Cet appartement est situé au dernier étage, au niveau du toit d'un entrepôt londonien du XIXe siècle. Les façades ont été laissées à l'état initial, la maçonnerie et les planchers mis en valeur. De nouvelles zones de services ont été installées près de la porte d'entrée. Le cahier des charges exigeait un appartement d'une chambre avec un bureau et une pièce polyvalente utilisable comme deuxième chambre, une fois fermée. Le concept optimise la sensation d'espace en déplaçant la porte d'entrée d'origine et créant une entrée à double hauteur, lien visuel entre les deux étages, qui donne accès à toutes les pièces. Un velux s'étend sur toute la longueur du dernier étage, inondant l'intérieur de lumière naturelle. Les grandes portes coulissantes et pivotantes ignifugées sont escamotables, conférant une grande fluidité entre les espaces ouverts salon/salle à manger/cuisine, tout en remplissant leur rôle en cas d'incendie.

Das Appartement befindet sich im Ober- und Dachgeschoss eines ehemaligen Londoner Lagerhauses aus dem 19. Jahrhundert. Die Fassaden blieben unverändert und die existierenden Ziegelmauern und Bodenfliesen wurden sichtbar belassen. Neue Servicebereiche entstanden nahe der Eingangstür. Der Kunde wünschte sich ein Schlafzimmer, ein Heimbüro und einen Mehrzweckraum, den man abtrennen und als zweites Schlafzimmer benutzen kann. Die Vordertür wurde verschoben und ein Korridor doppelter Höhe geschaffen, der die beiden Etagen visuell miteinander verbindet, alle Durchgangsbereiche umfasst und den Raum größer wirken lässt. Über dem Obergeschoss befindet sich ein Dachfenster, durch das Licht in die ganze Wohnung dringt. Die verschiedenen fahr- und schwenkbaren Feuertüren wurden verborgen, sodass ein fließender Übergang zwischen den offenen Bereichen entstand.

The most important of the new elements is the African-walnut wall panel, which extends from the open kitchen to the entrance hall and establishes a cohesive, predominantly natural feel.

La cloison en noyer d'Afrique, qui s'étend de la cuisine ouverte au hall d'entrée, est le plus important des nouveaux éléments, conférant à l'ensemble une impression d'unité avec une prédominance de la nature.

Das wichtigste neue Element ist das Wandelement aus afrikanischem Nussbaum, das von der offenen Küche bis zum Eingangsbereich reicht. So entsteht eine geschlossene, sehr natürliche Atmosphäre.

› Ground floor Rez-de-chaussée Erdgeschoss

› First floor Premier étage Erstes Obergeschoss

The bedroom is in one of the corners on the upper level. The terrace was covered with wooden sheets and has magnificent views of the city skyline.

La chambre se trouve dans l'un des angles de l'étage supérieur. La terrasse est revêtue de lattes de bois et offre une vue magnifique sur la ligne d'horizon de la ville.

Das Schlafzimmer befindet sich in einer der Ecken der oberen Etage. Die überdachte Terrasse, die eine wundervolle Aussicht über die Stadt bietet, ist mit Holzdielen ausgelegt.

A skylight runs the full length of the top floor, spreading natural light deep into the home.

Un velux court le long du toit, inondant toute la maison de lumière.

Über dem gesamten Obergeschoss befindet sich ein Dachfenster, durch das Licht in die ganze Wohnung dringt.

Brown Loft

Deborah Berke
New York, United States

An open plan, an emphasis on perspective and a muted palette of materials characterize this Soho loft. Part of a renovated industrial building, the space was fitted out for an artist and illustrator who wanted a space for living, working, and entertaining clients. The building's original columns were retained and restored, acting as a polished foil for the modernity of the renovation. Their presence creates an invisible line between the kitchen and living areas. Translucent acrylic and aluminum partitions allow for flexible divisions between the major spaces and disappear discreetly into pockets in the wall. A kitchen island was inserted into the open-plan space, acting simultaneously as a working surface, eating table, and divider between kitchen and living areas. Industrial attributes, such as the sprinkler pipes along the ceiling, were restored and kept exposed as a reminder of the building's original use.

Un plan ouvert, l'accent mis sur la perspective et un petit éventail de matériaux constituent les caractéristiques de ce loft de Soho. Partie d'un bâtiment industriel restauré, l'espace a été agencé pour un artiste illustrateur pour y vivre, y travailler et recevoir des clients. Les colonnes originales du bâtiment ont été gardées et restaurées, conférant tout son lustre à la modernité de la rénovation. Leur présence crée une ligne invisible entre la cuisine et les pièces à vivre. Cloisons en aluminium et acrylique translucide permettent de moduler les espaces principaux. Elles disparaissent discrètement dans des fentes murales. Un îlot central a été installé dans l'espace ouvert de la cuisine, faisant office à la fois de plan de travail, de table et de séparation entre la cuisine et les pièces à vivre. Les éléments d'usine, tels que des tuyaux d'arrosage au plafond, ont été restaurés et conservés en souvenir de l'édifice d'antan.

Offenheit, betonte Perspektiven und eine gegrenzte Materialpalette charakterisieren dieses Loft in Soho. In einem renovierten Fabrikgebäude sollten für die Auftraggeber, einen Künstler und einen Illustrator, Wohn- und Arbeitsräume sowie ein Gäste- und Kundenbereich geschaffen werden. Die vorhandenen Säulen wurden restauriert; sie dienen als eine Art aufpolierter Hintergrund für die Modernität der Renovierung und stellen eine Verbindung zwischen der Küche und den Wohnbereichen dar. Die Raumteiler aus lichtdurchlässigem Acryl und Aluminium dienen als variable Abgrenzungen zwischen den Hauptbereichen. In den offenen Raum wurde eine Kücheninsel integriert, die als Arbeitsfläche und Esstisch dient. Industrielle Elemente wie die Sprinklerrohre an der Decke wurden restauriert und blieben sichtbar, um an die Ursprünge des Gebäudes zu erinnern.

Translucent acrylic and aluminum partitions allow for flexible divisions between the main spaces but can disappear discreetly into pockets in the wall.

Des cloisons en acrylique translucide ou en aluminium permettent de moduler à souhait les espaces principaux et disparaissent rapidement dans des fentes murales.

Raumteiler aus lichtdurchlässigem Acryl und Aluminium dienen als variable Abgrenzungen zwischen den Hauptbereichen, sie können aber auch diskret in dafür vorgesehenen Wandöffnungen verborgen werden.

› **Plan** Plan Grundriss

Loft on Avenue Philippe Auguste

Laetitia Viallon and
Jean-François Piron
Paris, France

Situated in a quiet, sunny patio, this loft, originally part of a mirror store dating from 1920, was refurbished as a home and work space for a young couple without children. The redbrick building topped with a glass and metal structure, hampered by its limited size and lack of sunlight on part of the ground floor, required an intervention that concentrated on making the most of these restricted possibilities. Thus, the architects divided the space into a work studio, with the garden terrace on the ground floor, while the other rooms are on the first floor. The need to achieve the greatest possible space demanded the removal of barriers and opaque surfaces: the façade was made of glass, to capture the maximum amount of sunlight and extend the visual space of the interior into the patio dotted with trees. Moreover, the different areas are marked off by variations in the floor height, and by panels made of translucent or transparent materials.

Situé dans un patio calme et ensoleillé, ce loft faisait partie, à l'origine, d'une miroiterie de 1920. Il a été restauré en espace habitable et en bureau pour un couple sans enfants. Le bâtiment de briques rouges, coiffé d'une structure en verre et métal, souffrait de sa petite taille et du manque de lumière naturelle sur une partie du rez-de-chaussée. Le but de la restauration était d'optimiser cet espace malgré de faibles possibilités. Les architectes ont donc divisé l'espace en un studio faisant office de bureau, à côté du jardin terrasse au rez-de-chaussée. Les autres pièces se trouvent à l'étage. Le besoin impératif d'espace a nécessité le retrait de cloisons et de surfaces opaques : la nouvelle façade de verre permet de capter le maximum de soleil et de prolonger l'espace visuel de l'intérieur vers le patio arboré. En outre, les différentes zones sont délimitées par les différences de hauteur du sol et par des cloisons en matériaux translucides ou transparents.

Dieses Loft in einem ruhigen, sonnigen Hof war einst Teil eines Spiegelgeschäftes aus dem Jahr 1920. Es wurde zu einer Wohnung und einem Arbeitsraum für ein kinderloses Paar umgebaut. Das Gebäude aus rotem Ziegelstein ist relativ klein, und ein Teil des Erdgeschosses war sehr dunkel, was eine besondere Herausforderung für die Planer darstellte. Deshalb unterteilten die Architekten den Raum in ein Studio mit Gartenterrasse im Erdgeschoss und verlegten die anderen Räume in die erste Etage. Da möglichst viel Raum gewonnen werden musste, wurden viele Barrieren und lichtundurchlässige Oberflächen entfernt. Die Fassade ist aus Glas, um so viel Sonnenlicht wie möglich einzufangen und auch visuell den Raum in den baumbestandenen Innenhof auszudehnen. Die verschiedenen Bereiche werden durch unterschiedliche Fußbodenhöhen und Paneele aus lichtdurchlässigem oder transparentem Material voneinander abgegrenzt.

The different areas are marked off by both variations in the floor height and panels made of translucent or transparent materials.

Les différentes zones sont définies à la fois par les variations de hauteur des sols et par les cloisons translucides ou transparentes.

Die verschiedenen Zonen werden durch unterschiedliche Fußbodenhöhen und Paneele aus lichtdurchlässigem oder transparentem Material voneinander abgegrenzt.

› Ground floor Rez-de-chaussée Erdgeschoss

› First floor Premier étage Erstes Obergeschoss

› **Sections** Sections Schnitte

Marnix Warehouse

Fokkema Architecten
Antwerp, Belgium

Guided by the context of the project and the identity of their clients, these Belgian architects transformed a late-nineteenth-century warehouse into a dynamic living space. Situated on the northern edge of the city, next to a large harbor, this brick building had three major compartments constructed with oak beams and pine planks. Three cubes were created: the first floats above the ground floor and contains two bathrooms. The second, situated halfway up the loft, contains a bedroom and the kitchen. The third cube hangs from the ceiling and contains a crow's-nest bedroom. The cubes are not only functional but also mark out the circulation: cantilevered oak planks emerge from one of them as a staircase leading to the roof terrace. The abstract objects relate to each other through size and form, while the white plaster and translucent glass renew the old structure of wooden beams and pillars.

Guidés par la nature du projet et la personnalité des clients, ces architectes belges ont transformé un entrepôt de la fin du XIXe siècle, en un espace de vie dynamique. Situé dans la périphérie nord de la ville, près d'un grand port, ce bâtiment en briques est divisé en trois grands espaces principaux dotés de poutres en chêne et de madriers de pin. On a conçu trois cubes : le premier flotte au-dessus du rez-de-chaussée et comprend deux salles de bains. Le deuxième, au milieu du loft, abrite une chambre à coucher et une cuisine. Le troisième, suspendu au plafond tel un nid d'aigle, héberge une chambre à coucher. Outre leur rôle fonctionnel, les cubes servent à marquer le passage : une suspension en cantilever de madriers de chêne émerge de l'un d'eux, sous forme d'escalier menant au toit en terrasse. Forme et dimension relient les apports abstraits ; le plâtre blanc et le verre translucide créent un trait d'union avec l'ancienne structure de poutres et piliers de bois.

Die belgischen Architekten ließen sich vom Kontext des Gebäudes und der Persönlichkeit ihrer Kunden inspirieren, als sie dieses Lagerhaus aus dem 19. Jahrhundert in einen dynamischen Wohnraum umgestalteten. Das Ziegelsteingebäude mit drei großen Gebäudeteilen aus Eichenbalken und Kieferplanken befindet sich in der Nähe eines großen Hafens. Es wurden drei Würfel geschaffen. Der erste schwebt über dem Erdgeschoss und enthält die beiden Badezimmer. In dem zweiten auf halber Höhe sind ein Schlafzimmer und die Küche untergebracht. Der dritte hängt von der Decke und enthält ein Schlafzimmer im Stil eines Mastkorbes. Die Würfel sind funktionell und markieren die Wege durch den Wohnbereich. Aus einem der Würfel entspringen freitragende Eichenplanken als Treppe zur Dachterrasse. Die abstrakten Objekte stehen in Größe und Form miteinander in Verbindung. Weißer Gips und durchscheinendes Glas erneuern die alte Struktur.

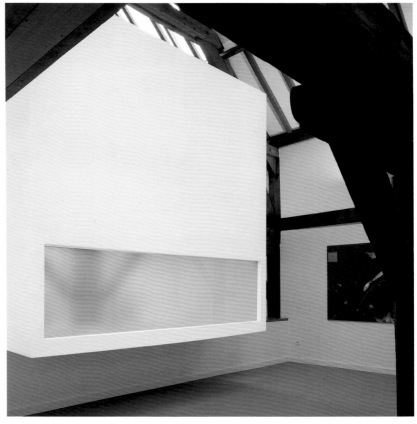

The cubes relate to each other through size and form, while the white plaster and translucent glass give new life to the old structure of wooden beams and pillars.

Les cubes sont liés les uns aux autres par leur taille et leur forme. Le plâtre blanc et le verre translucide créent un trait d'union avec l'ancienne structure articulée sur des poutres et des piliers de bois.

Die Würfel stehen in Größe und Form in Verbindung zueinander. Weißer Gips und durchscheinendes Glas erneuern die alte Struktur aus Holzbalken und Pfeilern.

› **Ground floor** Rez-de-chaussée Erdgeschoss

› **First floor** Premier étage Erstes Obergeschoss

The living room is an open space where sunshine can flow in through the light roof coverings.

Le salon est un espace ouvert où le soleil entre à flots par la structure légère de la couverture.

Das Wohnzimmer ist ein offener Raum und wird von Sonnenlicht durchströmt, das durch die helle Dachbedeckung fällt.

Sandblasted glass is the only barrier between the shower, which is placed in one of the cubes, and the adjoining living-room.

Le verre poli au jet de sable est le seul écran masquant la douche placée dans l'un des cubes, à côté du salon.

Die einzige Trennwand zwischen der in einem der Würfel befindlichen Dusche und dem angrenzenden Wohnzimmer ist aus sandgestrahltem Glas.

Loft in Venice

Owner
Venice, Italy

Located close to a large Venetian church, this loft was once an important nineteenth-century foundry. The restoration project (supervised by the owner himself) sought to maintain the existing structure while transforming the space into a home that would respond to the needs of its tenants. The considerable height of the ceiling made it possible to insert a mezzanine that acts as a catwalk, offering views of the church dome and the stone-paved patio. The wood-and-metal staircase leads down to a small studio, which is partitioned off from the surrounding living and dining areas. All the installations are concealed beneath the birchwood floors. The furnishings were designed by the owner, except for the sixteenth-century Iberian monetiere. Solid wooden trusses, brick walls and glass doors guarantee a translucent space full of character in this post-industrial loft in Venice.

A deux pas d'une église vénitienne, ce loft est une ancienne fonderie du XIXe siècle. Le projet de rénovation (conduit par le propriétaire en personne) visait à conserver la structure en place tout en la transformant en une demeure adaptée aux besoins de ses occupants. La hauteur considérable du plafond permet d'y intégrer une mezzanine, à l'instar d'une passerelle permettant de voir le toit de l'église et le patio pavé. L'escalier, une conjugaison de bois et de fer, conduit à un petit studio, séparé du salon et de la salle à manger. Tous les équipements sont cachés sous les sols en bois de bouleau. Le propriétaire a dessiné les meubles, à l'exception d'une bonnetière espagnole du XVIe siècle. Poutres en bois massif, murs de brique et portes en verre confèrent transparence et originalité à ce loft post-industriel de Venise.

Dieses Loft in der Nähe einer großen venezianischen Kirche war im 19. Jahrhundert eine bedeutende Gießerei. Bei der Renovierung, die vom Eigentümer selbst beaufsichtigt wurde, versuchte man, die existierende Struktur zu erhalten und gleichzeitig den Raum in ein Zuhause zu verwandeln, das den Bedürfnissen seiner Bewohner entspricht. Aufgrund der außergewöhnlich hohen Decke konnte ein Zwischengeschoss eingefügt werden, von dem aus man einen guten Blick auf die Kirche und den mit Stein gepflasterten Innenhof hat. Die Treppe aus Holz und Metall führt in ein kleines Studio, das von den umgebenden Wohn- und Essbereichen abgetrennt ist. Alle Installationen sind unter den Birkenholzböden verborgen. Bis auf den iberischen Münzschrank aus dem 16. Jahrhundert sind alle Möbel vom Eigentümer selbst entworfen. Solides Holzfachwerk, Ziegelwände und Glastüren machen dieses postindustrielle Loft in Venedig zu einem eigenwilligen, hellen Raum.

A combination of Asian style and Italian tradition characterizes this loft designed by an antique collector.

L'alliance de style asiatique et de la tradition italienne définit ce loft conçu par un collectionneur d'antiquités

Eine Kombination des asiatischen Stils mit italienischer Tradition charakterisiert dieses Loft, das von einem Antiquitätensammler gestaltet wurde.

The dining area and adjacent courtyard are examples of the Asian influence on the design, while the kitchen illustrates the Italian style.

Le design de la salle à manger et de la cour adjacente reflète l'influence asiatique, tandis que la cuisine relève du style italien.

Der Essbereich und der anliegende Hof sind Beispiele für den asiatischen Einfluss, während die Küche ganz klar im italienischen Stil gehalten ist.

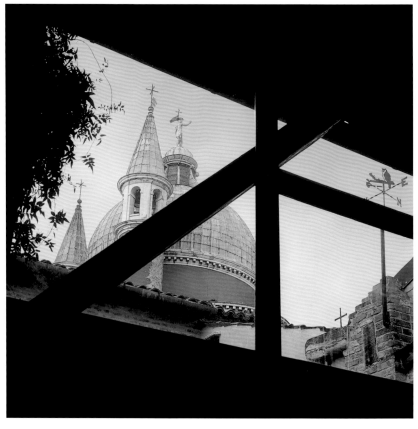

The interior of the loft provides a beautiful view of the beautiful basilica nearby.

L'intérieur du loft s'ouvre sur la vue magnifique de la basilique proche.

Vom Inneren des Lofts aus hat man einen wundervollen Blick auf die benachbarte Basilika.

Loft on Rue Bichat

Beres Platane
Paris, France

The architect responsible for the restoration of this old two-story warehouse sought to maintain the existing structure without making any modification to its façades. This led to the idea of accentuating the contrast between the existing structure and the additions. The first step was to highlight the structure by endowing it with playful shapes and bright colors, thereby emphasizing its presence and calling attention to its use. Another determining factor of the intervention was the maximum possible exploitation of natural light. The façade was stripped of any elements that disturbed the flow of light and a large, diamond-shape window was installed to distribute the illumination. Furthermore, the empty space under the staircase was used as a means of allowing light to penetrate into the interior.

L'architecte responsable de la restauration de cet entrepôt à deux étages a essayé de maintenir la structure préexistante sans en modifier les façades. L'idée était de souligner le contraste entre cette structure existante et les parties ajoutées. Il s'agissait avant tout d'accentuer la structure en la parant de formes ludiques aux couleurs vives pour en exalter l'aspect et la fonction. Le programme de restauration s'est ensuite consacré à l'exploitation maximum de la lumière naturelle. La façade est libérée de tout élément gênant par une grande fenêtre en forme de diamant qui distribue la lumière. En outre, le vide sous l'escalier est utilisé pour laisser pénétrer la lumière à l'intérieur.

Der Architekt, der dieses ehemalige zweigeschossige Lagerhaus renovierte, wollte die existierende Struktur bewahren, ohne die Fassaden zu verändern. So kam er auf die Idee, den Kontrast zwischen der vorhandenen Struktur und den hinzugefügten Elementen zu unterstreichen. Zunächst wurde die Struktur betont, indem man sie mit verspielten Formen und hellen Farben versah. So wurde ihre Präsenz hervorgehoben und die Aufmerksamkeit auf sie gelenkt. Außerdem sollte das Tageslicht so weit wie möglich ausgenutzt werden. Die Fassade wurde von allen Elementen befreit, die das Einfallen des Lichtes behinderten, und man schuf ein großes, rautenförmiges Fenster, das das Licht verteilt. Außerdem wurde der leere Raum unter der Treppe dazu benutzt, Tageslicht ins Innere dringen zu lassen.

The project has created an environment in which the placement of objects determines the use of each setting, so that functionality is closely linked to the visual effect.

Le projet a créé un environnement dans lequel l'emplacement des objets détermine la fonction de chaque espace. Fonctionnalité et impact visuel y sont étroitement liés.

Hier wurde eine Umgebung geschaffen, in der der Einsatz von Objekten die Nutzung der Räume bestimmt, sodass die Funktionalität eng mit der visuellen Wirkung verbunden ist.

› Second floor   Deuxième étage   Zweites Obergeschoss

› First floor   Premier étage   Erstes Obergeschoss

› Ground floor   Rez-de-chaussée   Erdgeschoss

› Section   Section   Schnitt

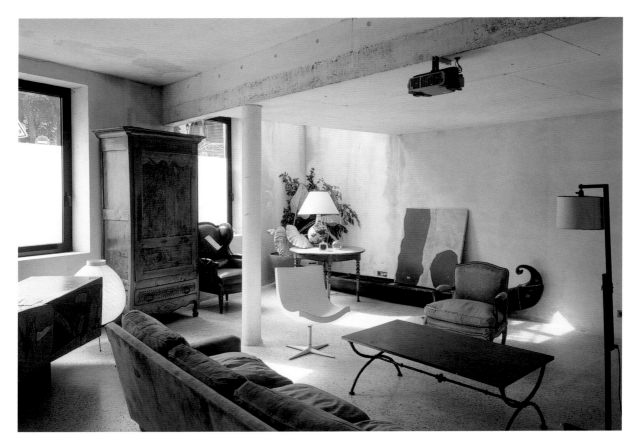

The façade was stripped of any elements that impeded the flow of light and fitted with a large window, with an uneven shape designed to distribute light more effectively.

La facciata è stata spogliata di tutti gli elementi che disturbavano il flusso di luce, mentre una finestra dalla forma insolita distribuisce l'illuminazione in modo ottimale.

Alle Elemente, die den Einfall des Lichtes behinderten, wurden von der Fassade entfernt, und man schuf ein großes Fenster, das das Licht noch effektiver verteilt.

› **Perspectives** Perspectives Perspektiven

House inside a House

Giovanni Longo
Milan, Italy

Once the site of a big factory, this attic space was refurbished to create a living space for a young professional. The architectural elements, chosen for their contrasting volumes with respect to their function, establish the different areas within a fluid, open-plan space. The living room occupies the central area. A chimney that pierces the ceiling delineates the kitchen and dining area, which lie underneath a lowered ceiling that stops short on either side to receive a skylight. The vertical void above the kitchen is intersected by a glass panel that serves as a walkway on the attic level. A steel staircase leads to the bedroom, which is sheltered inside an independent structure for ultimate privacy and an escape from daily routine. Vintage and antique furniture mingle effortlessly with both ordinary and designer pieces, adding a great deal of character and personality to the home.

Cet espace sous les toits, jadis une ancienne usine, a été rénové pour devenir le logement d'un jeune professionnel. Les éléments architecturaux sélectionnés pour leurs volumes, alliant contraste et respect des fonctions, définissent les différentes zones selon un concept d'espace ouvert et fluide Le salon occupe la zone centrale. La cheminée perce le plafond et délimite ainsi la cuisine et la salle à manger située sous un plafond surbaissé, ouvert à chaque bout, pour laisser passer un puits de lumière. Le vide vertical au-dessus de la cuisine est interrompu par un panneau de verre qui sert de passage au niveau de la mansarde. Un escalier d'acier dessert la chambre protégée par une structure indépendante pour préserver au maximum l'intimité et rompre avec la routine quotidienne. Le mobilier ancien et classique s'unit parfaitement aux meubles ordinaires ou design, exaltant à merveille le caractère et la personnalité de l'habitation.

Dieses Dachgeschoss, einst eine große Fabriketage, wurde zu einer Wohnung für ein junges Paar umgebaut. Die architektonischen Elemente, die aufgrund ihrer unterschiedlichen Volumen für die jeweiligen Funktionen gewählt wurden, bilden verschiedene Zonen in einem offenen Raum. Das Wohnzimmer befindet sich im Zentrum. Ein Kamin durchbohrt die Decke und begrenzt Küche und Essbereich, die unter einer abgehängten Decke liegen, in der sich auf beiden Seiten ein Oberlicht befindet. Der Hohlraum oberhalb der Küche wird von einer Glasplatte unterbrochen, die als Laufsteg der oberen Ebene dient. Eine Stahltreppe führt zum Schlafzimmer, das sich innerhalb einer unabhängigen Struktur befindet, ein Ort, um sich von der täglichen Routine zurückzuziehen. Alte, antike Möbel werden völlig ungezwungen mit außergewöhnlichen Elementen und Designermöbeln kombiniert, was diesem Zuhause einen ganz besonderen Charakter verleiht.

Lightweight elements like the minimal staircase and glass catwalk maintain the spacious character of this industrial loft.

Des éléments légers, à l'instar de l'escalier minimaliste et de la passerelle de verre, préservent l'espace de ce loft industriel.

Leichte Elemente wie die kleine Treppe und der Laufsteg aus Glas unterstreichen den weitläufigen Charakter dieser Fabriketage.

› Ground floor Rez-de-chaussée Erdgeschoss

› Mezzanine Mezzanine Zwischengeschoss

› Sections Sections Schnitte

The kitchen is both practical and attractive. Its U-shape allows for appliances to be kept out of sight of the living and dining area.

La cuisine décline commodité et beauté. Sa forme en U permet de maintenir les équipements hors de la vue de la salle à manger et du salon.

Die Küche ist praktisch und schön. Alle Geräte sind U-förmig angeordnet, sodass sie vom Wohn- und Essbereich aus nicht sichtbar sind.

Black Box

Weysen + De Baere
Ghent, Belgium

The old docks at Ghent were in a dilapidated state after centuries of industrial usage. However, an ambitious city renewal program has transformed this zone. This has created an outlet for ambitious projects like this old factory, dating from the second half of the 19th century, which has been converted into a dwelling. Due to the thin budget, the architects sought a building they themselves could renovate. Their aim was to conciliate the grandeur of the old factory with modern living requirements. They opted for a 3.50 x 18 m box-shaped volume, designed in line with the existing metal structure. The box's position and openings are variable and can be adapted to owners' needs and the changing seasons. The result is a bold, modern design that is strikingly self-assured.

Les vieux quais de Gante étaient dans un sévère état de détérioration dû à leur longue utilisation industrielle. Grâce à un ambitieux projet de rénovation de la ville, ce quartier a été réhabilité afin de laisser place à des projets comme celui-ci qui transforme une ancienne usine datant de la deuxième moitié du XIXème siècle en maison. En raison du budget limité, les architectes ont cherché un bâtiment qu'eux-mêmes pourraient réhabiliter, en essayant de concilier les volumes d'une ancienne usine aux nécessités actuelles d'une maison. Pour cela, ils ont opté pour un volume en forme de caisse de 3,50 x 18 m de superficie, modulable en fonction de la structure métallique existante. L'emplacement et les ouvertures de la boîte varient et s'adaptent aux nécessités des propriétaires, et aux changements climatiques de chaque saison. Le résultat : un concept moderne et osé qui attire l'attention pour sa désinvolture.

Das ehemalige Hafengebiet in Gent befand sich nach Jahrzehnten industrieller Nutzung in sehr schlechtem Zustand. Dank eines ehrgeizigen Erneuerungsprojekts der Stadt wurde das Gebiet restauriert, um Projekte wie das hier gezeigte zu ermöglichen. In diesem Fall wurde eine alte Fabrik aus der zweiten Hälfte des 19. Jahrhunderts in Wohnraum umgewandelt. Aufgrund des niedrigen Budgets suchten die Architekten ein Gebäude, das sie selbst restaurieren konnten. Dabei versuchten sie, die Erhabenheit einer alten Fabrik mit dem heutigen Wohnbedarf zu vereinen. Zu diesem Zweck entschieden sie sich für ein großes Volumen in Kastenform auf einer Grundfläche von 3,50 x 18 m, das im Einklang mit der vorhandenen Metallstruktur umgesetzt werden sollte. Platzierung und Öffnungen des Kastens sind variabel, sodass sie sich an die Bedürfnisse der Besitzer und die Klimaänderungen der einzelnen Jahreszeiten anpassen. Das Ergebnis ist ein modernes und gewagtes Design, das aufgrund seiner Ungezwungenheit Aufsehen erregt.

› Plan Plan Grundriss

› Sections Sections Schnitte

The different black structural modular panels are storage spaces and also delimit the routes between the different areas of the loft.

Les différents panneaux modulaires de la structure de couleur noire servent d'espaces de rangement et permettent de délimiter les différents espaces du loft.

Die einzelnen schwarzen Strukturmodulpaneele dienen als Aufbewahrungsbereiche und helfen gleichzeitig dabei, die Wege zwischen den verschiedenen Loftbereichen zu kennzeichnen.

Wagner Loft

Michael Carapetian
Venice, Italy

This residence was inserted into an industrial shell that was originally built in 1910 and known as the Dreher Brewery. The architect's aim was to keep the structure intact by introducing new floors to hold up the rooms without removing any of the existing brick walls and wood trusses. The terraces and the lower level of the loft are raised by a suspended steel floor and a suspended steel frame wall, dividing the space from the rest of the surrounding structure. A stainless-steel staircase, consisting of single steps made of glass and steel sheets, guides the circulation throughout the space and ends up in the sleeping gallery, which contains a suspended, circular bath tub, a shower and a glass toilet cubicle. The wooden deck terrace is made up of paths and small ponds, providing an ideal place to relax and enjoy the views of Venice in the distance.

Le complexe industriel construit en 1910, connu sous le nom de Brasserie Dreher, abrite cette nouvelle résidence. L'architecte a voulu garder la structure préexistante. Il y a ajouté de nouveaux sols, conservant ainsi les pièces sans toucher aux anciens murs de briques ni à la charpente de bois. Les terrasses et la partie inférieure du loft sont soutenues par un sol d'acier et un mur porteur suspendus séparant l'espace du reste de la structure. Un escalier en acier inoxydable, constitué de marches individuelles en verre et feuilles d'aluminium, traverse l'espace pour aboutir à la galerie dortoir, dotée d'une baignoire circulaire suspendue, d'une douche et d'un lavabo de verre. La terrasse de bois est ponctuée de passages et de petits étangs, lieu idyllique pour se détendre et jouir des vues sur Venise qui se profile à l'horizon.

Dieses Wohnambiente befindet sich in der Dreher-Brauerei, einem Industriegebäude aus dem Jahr 1910. Ziel des Architekten war es, die bestehende Struktur zu erhalten. Dazu konstruierte er neue Böden, die die Räume stützen, ohne dazu das existierende Fachwerk und die Ziegelwände entfernen zu müssen. Die Terrassen und das Erdgeschoss wurden auf einem hängenden Stahlboden und mit einer Wand aus Stahlrahmen konstruiert und trennen den Raum von der umgebenden Struktur ab. Eine Edelstahltreppe mit Glas- und Stahlplatten führt durch die Räume zur Schlafgalerie, in der sich eine hängende runde Badewanne, eine Dusche und eine Toilettenzelle aus Glas befinden. Über die holzbelegte Dachterrasse führen Pfade und kleine Brücken, und sie dient als idealer Ort zum Entspannen, von dem aus man Venedig in der Ferne sieht.

The asymmetrical fireplace and supporting steel columns are among the various sculptural elements that give character to the home.

La cheminée asymétrique et les colonnes portantes en acier sont quelques-uns des éléments sculpturaux qui caractérisent ce lieu.

Der asymmetrische Kamin und die Stützsäulen aus Stahl sind einige der verschiedenen, skulpturellen Elemente, die diesem Zuhause einen besonderen Charakter verleihen.

On the top floor, a free-standing shower separates the bedroom from the bathroom area.

A l'étage supérieur, une douche autoportante sépare la chambre de la salle de bains.

Im Obergeschoss trennt eine freistehende Dusche das Schlafzimmer vom Badezimmer ab.

The exterior of this house, which reflects its industrial origins, has been transformed into an Italian villa with the help of a meticulously landscaped garden.

L'extérieur de cette maison, qui reflète ses origines industrielles, a été transformé en une villa italienne grâce à un remodelage méticuleux du jardin.

Von außen verlieh man diesem Haus, dem man seine industriellen Ursprünge noch ansieht, durch einen sorgfältig gestalteten Garten das Flair einer italienischen Villa.

Loft in Brooklyn

Delson or Sherman
Architects
New York, United States

This former warehouse was converted into a church in the 1930s. The architects bought the neglected property and transformed it into a home for a family of four. The space was gutted, although even the shell was in need of repair. Major structural work included rebuilding an exterior wall and bolstering existing trusses with new heavy-timber struts and steel plates. In order to emphasize the immense two-story volume, a series of deep skylights was installed into the ceiling to flood the space with light. The industrial character of the space was maintained, leaving the new masonry wall exposed and painting the stripped floors. The mezzanine, once the church's choir stalls, contains an intimate living area and shelters another lounge underneath, offering cozy alternatives to the main room. The stainless-steel kitchen is a welcome contrast to the loft's wooden framework.

Dans les années 30, cet ancien entrepôt a été reconverti en église. Après l'achat de cette propriété délaissée, les architectes l'ont restructurée en résidence pour une famille de quatre personnes. L'espace était vide et l'ossature même devait être réparée. Il fallut entreprendre de sérieux travaux de structure, notamment reconstruire l'extérieur et renforcer les poutres existantes par de nouveaux arcs-boutants de bois et des plaques d'acier. Pour mettre en valeur ce volume réparti sur deux niveaux, une série de velux a été installée dans le toit, inondant ainsi l'espace de lumière. Grâce au nouveau mur en maçonnerie brute et aux sols striés peints, ce bâtiment conserve son cachet de bâtiment industriel. La mezzanine, à l'emplacement des anciennes stalles d'église, est dotée d'une salle de séjour et abrite un autre salon en dessous, une alternative conviviale et confortable à la pièce principale. La cuisine en inox contraste agréablement avec la charpente de bois du loft.

Dieses ehemalige Lagerhaus wurde 1930 in eine Kirche umgewandelt. Die Architekten kauften den vernachlässigten Besitz und schufen ein Zuhause für eine vierköpfige Familie. Das Haus wurde entkernt, obwohl sogar die Fassade sanierungsbedürftig war. Zu diesen großen Strukturarbeiten gehörten der Wiederaufbau der Außenmauer und das Stützen des originalen Hängewerks. Um die Höhe des zweistöckigen Raumes zu unterstreichen, strömt Sonnenlicht durch eine Reihe tiefer Dachfenster in alle Winkel. Der industrielle Charakter des Gebäudes blieb erhalten, die neu gemauerte Wand blieb unverputzt und die freigelegten Fußböden wurden gestrichen. Im Zwischengeschoss, wo einst der Chor der Kirche war, entstand ein intimer Wohnbereich mit einem darunter liegenden zweiten Wohnzimmer, sodass man über zwei gemütliche Gesellschaftszimmer verfügt. Die Küche aus Edelstahl bildet einen angenehmen Gegensatz zu den Holzbalken.

A series of deep skylights were installed into the ceiling to allow light to spill into the space, while the room was furnished with a giant 20-ft. table and long bookcases.

Une série de grands velux a été installée dans le plafond pour permettre à la lumière d'inonder l'espace. La pièce est dotée d'une table géante de 6 m de long et d'une bibliothèque tout en longueur.

Es wurden eine Reihe von tiefen Dachfenstern in der Decke installiert, sodass der ganze Raum, der mit einem riesigen, 6 m langen Tisch und langen Bücherregalen möbliert ist, von Tageslicht überflutet wird.

› **First floor** Premier étage Erstes Obergeschoss   › **Ground floor** Rez-de-chaussée Erdgeschoss   › **Basement** Sous-sol Kellergeschoss

Schein Loft

Archi-Tectonics
Soho, New York, USA

Nestled in a corner of Soho, this old six-story warehouse has been transformed into a build-ing housing 11 loft apartments. The entrance to this apartment opens onto the shorter end of a L-shaped space. In the west-facing wall, the floor-to-ceiling windows are the central feature, providing breathtaking views over the surrounding area. Another pivotal element is the oak unit running throughout most of the apartment. In addition to providing ample storage space, this unit also divides the different living spaces. The grains in this polished unit give many of its surfaces a striped appearance, creating a strong visual impact. The architect explained how the owner's willingness to adopt sculptural forms allowed her to let her creativity run wild. The results are spectacular.

Situé dans le quartier de Soho, un ancien magasin de 6 étages s'est reconverti en un bâti-ment constitué de 11 lofts. L'entrée de cet appartement est reliée à la partie extrême d'un étage en forme de L. A l'ouest, les impressionnantes vues ont le rôle principal grâce aux baies vitrées qui vont du sol au plafond. Le module en bois de chêne est un autre élément fondamental de l'appartement. Ce module couvre une grande partie de l'étage et, outre le fait de séparer les pièces, il offre de vastes espaces de rangement. Les veines cirées de ce revê-tement donnent à de nombreuses superficies un aspect tigré, dont l'impact visuel est impres-sionnant. Selon l'architecte, le propriétaire était d'accord pour utiliser des formes structu-relles, ce qui lui a permis de laisser cours à sa créativité qui a conduit à des résultats spectaculaires.

Eine alte, sechsstöckige Lagerhalle in Soho beherbergt heute ein Gebäude mit 11 Lofts. Der Eingang zu diesem Appartement ist mit dem kurzen Ende eines L-förmigen Grundrisses ver-bunden. Richtung Westen gebührt die Hauptrolle der beeindruckenden Aussicht durch die vom Boden bis zur Decke reichenden Glaswände. Ein weiteres grundlegendes Element die-ses Appartements ist das Eichenholzmodul, das einen großen Teil des Grundrisses einnimmt und sowohl als großer Aufbewahrungsbereich wie auch als Raumteiler dient. Die mit Wachs behandelten Maserungen der Holzverkleidung verleihen vielen Flächen ein getigertes Aussehen mit enormer optischer Wirkung. Der Architektin zufolge war der Besitzer offen für den Einsatz bildhauerischer Formen, sodass sie ihrer Kreativität freien Lauf ließ und damit spektakuläre Ergebnisse erzielte.

The profusion of light flooding through the glass window projects intense shades on the surfaces, such as the dark gray painted walls and the oak unit that has darker hues ingrained in the wood.

La baie vitrée favorise l'abondante luminosité qui rend les superficies extrêmement teintées, comme par exemple les murs peints en gris foncé et le bois de chêne qui présente également des zones plus obscures.

Die durch die Glaswand eindringende Fülle an Tageslicht ermöglicht intensive Farbtöne auf den Wandflächen, wie zum Beispiel einen dunkelgrauen Anstrich oder dunkles Eichenholz.

› **Section** Section Schnitt

Taffer Loft

Audrey Matlock Architects
New York, United States

Audrey Matlock Architects restored one floor of an industrial complex on the shore of the Hudson River, and converted it into a home for a couple. As the clients did not require too intimate a space, the project envisioned a house with an open layout. Although the different areas are sometimes divided, they always maintain a certain relationship with one another, thanks to mobile partitions. Some of these are partially translucent, as they are inset with a glass upper section, while others do not reach the ceiling and consist of wooden or treated glass panels set within a steel frame and fitted with wheels that slide along rails in the ceiling or floor. The concrete structure has been preserved and is visible in the ceilings and columns. As an esthetic counterpoint, some of the walls were painted white and others were covered with maple wood.

Le bureau d'architectes Audrey Matlock a restauré l'étage d'un complexe industriel sur les berges de la rivière Hudson et l'a converti en un logement pour un couple. A la requête des clients, peu axés sur l'intimité, la maison a été conçue comme un espace ouvert. Même si les différentes zones sont parfois divisées, elles gardent toujours une certaine corrélation, grâce à des cloisons amovibles. Certaines d'entre elles sont translucides, dotées d'une partie supérieure en verre, d'autres ne vont pas jusqu'au plafond et sont faites de panneaux en bois ou en verre traité, insérés dans un cadre de métal monté sur roulettes et glissant dans un rail fixé au plafond ou au sol. Le béton est conservé et visible sur les colonnes ou au plafond. Points d'orgue esthétiques, certains murs sont peints en blanc ou habillés de bois d'érable.

Audrey Matlock Architects setzten eine Etage eines Industriegebäudes am Ufer des Hudson Rivers instand und machten daraus ein Zuhause für ein Ehepaar. Da die Kunden sich keine allzu intimen Räume wünschten, wurde das Haus sehr offen angelegt. Obwohl die verschiedenen Bereiche teilweise unterteilt sind, stehen sie immer zueinander in Beziehung, da die Raumteiler beweglich sind. Einige davon sind durch den Einsatz von Glasstreifen im oberen Bereich lichtdurchlässig. Andere reichen bis zur Decke und bestehen aus Holz- oder behandelten Glasplatten in einem Stahlrahmen auf Rädern, die über Schienen im Boden und an der Decke verschoben werden. Die Betonstruktur blieb erhalten und ist in der Decke und den Säulen noch sichtbar. Um einen ästhetischen Kontrapunkt zu schaffen, sind einige der Wände weiß gestrichen und andere mit Ahornholz verkleidet.

A motorized system of lightweight white drapes offers intimacy and regulates the entrance of natural light; they can be taken down and hidden behind the radiators.

Un système de tentures légères et blanches, à commande électrique, permet de créer une certaine intimité et de régler le flux de lumière naturelle. Démontables, elles sont faciles à dissimuler derrière les radiateurs.

Durch ein elektrisch steuerbares System aus leichten, weißen Stoffen können die Räume abgeteilt und das Einfallen des Tageslichts reguliert werden. Die Stoffe können ganz heruntergelassen und hinter den Heizkörpern verborgen werden.

The enormous windows in the kitchen provide ample light and magnificent views of the surroundings. The small table serves for informal meals and breakfasts.

Les immenses baies vitrées de la cuisine permettent à la lumière d'entrée en abondance et offrent des vues splendides sur les alentours. La petite table sert aux repas et petits déjeuners en famille.

Die Küchenfenster sind riesig, sodass viel Licht einfällt und man einen wundervollen Blick auf die Umgebung hat. Der kleine Tisch wird zum Frühstücken und anderen zwanglosen Mahlzeiten benutzt.

Loft at Prenzlauer Berg

Four young people rented this loft in the Prenzlauer Berg neighborhood, situated in what was once East Berlin, and converted it into their home. It is set in an old post office building that had been abandoned for five years. The old administrative offices on the first floor were divided into four private rooms, a large communal space with a kitchen and living-room, and a multipurpose hall with ranks of bookshelves and a dining room. The interior decoration took full advantage of the existing fittings and party walls. A tight budget can sometimes lead to poorly designed and uninviting spaces; in this case, imagination and ingenuity more than compensated for any shortage of money and the result is a warm, comfortable home. The lamps, for example, consist of old illuminated signs, while the furniture is an amusing mix of second-hand or recycled objects, such as the bed with a base of bricks covered with a wooden plank.

Quatre jeunes ont loué ce loft à Prenzlauer Berg ancien quartier de Berlin Est dans une vieille poste abandonnée depuis cinq ans, pour y élire domicile. Les anciens bureaux administratifs, au premier étage, ont été divisés en quatre parties privées, un vaste espace commun doté d'une cuisine et d'un salon, un hall d'entrée polyvalent garni d'étagères et une salle à manger. L'agencement existant et les cloisons initiales ont servi de base à la décoration intérieure. En général, les budgets serrés ne sont pas synonymes d'espaces design et accueillants. Dans ce cas précis et en dépit des faibles moyens, le mariage de l'ingéniosité et de l'imagination a réussi à créer un logement confortable et chaleureux. Les lampes, par exemple, sont d'anciennes enseignes lumineuses, l'ameublement est un méli-mélo sympathique d'objets d'occasion ou recyclés, tel le lit constitué d'un socle de briques recouvert d'une planche de bois.

Vier junge Leute mieteten dieses Loft am Prenzlauer Berg, ehemals Ostberlin, um es in ihr Zuhause zu verwandeln. Es befindet sich in einem alten, seit fünf Jahren leer stehenden Postgebäude. Die ehemalige Post im Erdgeschoss wurde in vier private Räume, einen großen Gemeinschaftsraum mit Küche und Wohnzimmer, einen Mehrzweckraum mit Bücherregalen und ein Esszimmer unterteilt. Bei der Innengestaltung wurden die existierenden Verbindungen und Wände einbezogen. Wenn wenig Geld zur Verfügung steht, führt dies manchmal zu ärmlich wirkenden, ungemütlichen Räumen. In diesem Fall aber wurde der Mangel an finanziellen Mitteln durch einen immensen Einfallsreichtum wettgemacht, sodass ein warmes und gastliches Zuhause entstand. Die Lampen zum Beispiel sind alte Leuchtreklamen, und das Mobiliar ist eine amüsante Mischung aus Objekten aus zweiter Hand und recycelten Elementen wie dem Bett, das aus einer Basis aus Ziegelsteinen und einer Holzplatte besteht.

The combination of different types of furniture and decorative elements (antiques, secondhand pieces, paintings and prints, and illuminated signs) makes for an eclectic and warm setting.

L'alliance de différentes sortes de meubles et divers éléments de décoration (antiquités, meubles d'occasion, peintures, gravures et enseignes lumineuses) engendre un agencement aussi chaleureux qu'éclectique.

Die Kombination verschiedener Möbeltypen und Dekorationselemente (Antiquitäten, Gegenstände aus zweiter Hand, Gemälde, Drucke und Leuchtschilder) lässt das Loft eklektisch und warm wirken.

Loft in Lombardia

Massimo Imparato
& Mauro Manfrin/BauQ
Milan, Italy

The studio BauQ transformed this 1920s' industrial warehouse into a home for an artist, a textile designer and their daughter. The elongated shape of the space and its high ceilings impelled the architects to divide it lengthwise and create a mezzanine that serves as a studio. A half-height white panel was used for this purpose, ensuring a visual continuity within the space and avoiding a rigid separation between the two areas. A metal grated staircase leads up to the studio, which was made with prefabricated white cement slabs laid over a metal structure. Beyond the stairs and a translucent screen, the kitchen and dining area share a common space, which leads on to the daughter's bedroom. A full-height window fills the lively and playful room with natural light during the day. The framework of wooden beams on the roof structure is the most notable architectural feature of the loft and dates back to the 1950s.

Le Studio BauQ a transformé cet entrepôt industriel des années 20, en une maison d'artiste, pour un designer textile et sa fille. La forme allongée de l'espace et ses hauts plafonds ont amené les architectes à le diviser dans le sens de la longueur et à créer une mezzanine qui serve de studio. Un panneau blanc à mi-hauteur permet une continuité visuelle au cœur de l'espace, évitant la séparation stricte des deux zones. Un escalier de métal grillagé conduit au studio, réalisé en placoplâtre posé sur une ossature de métal. Cachées derrière l'escalier et un paravent translucide, la cuisine et la salle à manger se partagent l'espace qui mène à la chambre de la fille. Une fenêtre, couvrant toute la hauteur, inonde de lumière du jour la pièce gaie et ludique. La charpente en bois, des années 50, est le plus bel élément architectural, image de marque du loft.

Das Studio BauQ baute dieses Lagerhaus aus den 1920er-Jahren in ein Heim für eine Künstlerfamilie (Künstler, Textildesigner und Tochter) um. Der lange Raum mit den hohen Decken brachte den Architekten auf die Idee, ihn der Länge nach aufzuteilen und ein Zwischengeschoss zu schaffen, das als Atelier dient. Dazu wurde ein weißes Paneel halber Höhe benutzt, sodass die visuelle Kontinuität des Raumes bewahrt wurde, da keine starre Trennung der beiden Bereiche notwendig war. Eine Treppe aus Metallgitter führt zum Atelier, das aus vorgefertigten Zementplatten über einer Metallstruktur konstruiert wurde. Hinter der Treppe und einem lichtdurchlässigen Schirm teilen sich Küche und Essbereich den Raum, der zum Schlafzimmer der Tochter führt. Ein deckenhohes Fenster lässt das Tageslicht in diesen lebendigen und verspielten Raum strömen. Das interessanteste architektonische Element dieses Lofts ist das Holzfachwerk des Daches aus den 1950er-Jahren.

Brick pillars mark the transition from public to private areas. Just behind, a metal grated staircase leads to the artist's studio.

Des colonnes de briques délimitent les zones privées et publiques entre elles. Juste derrière, un escalier en grille métallique mène au studio de l'artiste.

Ziegelsteinsäulen markieren den Übergang von den öffentlichen zu den privaten Bereichen. Dahinter führt eine Treppe aus Metallgitter zum Künstleratelier.

› Ground floor Rez-de-chaussée Erdgeschoss

› First floor Premier étage Erstes Obergeschoss

The most notable architectural feature of the loft is the framework of wooden beams, which is completed with a skylight that enables sunshine to penetrate within the space.

La structure de la charpente du toit en poutres de bois, complétée par un velux qui permet au soleil d'inonder l'espace, est l'élément architectural le plus remarquable du loft.

Das bemerkenswerteste Element dieses Lofts ist das Holzfachwerk der Dachstruktur, in der durch ein Oberlicht die Sonne in den Raum dringt.

Loft in Brussels

Luc Binst
Brussels, Belgium

This loft preserves the essential aspects of its former life, especially in terms of its floor plan layout. In addition to this, the design embodies several elements that are key to the "urban living" concept. The depth of the space, which is in essence elongated, is accentuated by the catwalk that has been configured between the different zones. Walls that would interrupt the space have been substituted for a steel, stepped box that marks out the space containing the dining area/conference table. This box also forms the kitchen space where the utensils are neatly concealed behind a large metal unit. At one end, a series of glass panels awash with violet light help to delimit the bedroom and bathroom spaces, without compromising in any way the transparency of the transit routes.

Ce loft conserve les aspects fondamentaux de la construction précédente, notamment concernant la distribution de l'étage. De plus, le concept souligne quelques éléments qui ont une incidence sur l'idée de « vie urbaine ». La profondeur de l'espace, déjà allongé, est accentuée par les superficies ouvertes conçues entre les différents espaces. L'absence de murs qui coupent l'étage est remplacée par une caisse en acier échelonnée qui aide à délimiter l'espace salle à manger/table de réunions. Cet espace sert également de cuisine, dont les ustensiles sont cachés derrière une grande console métallique. A l'autre extrémité, une série de panneaux en verre éclairés par une lumière violette permet de séparer la chambre à coucher de la salle de bains sans enlever la moindre clarté aux espaces.

Dieses Loft bewahrt grundlegende Eigenschaften seiner vorherigen Nutzung, und zwar hauptsächlich hinsichtlich der Grundrissaufteilung. Zusätzlich sollten einige Elemente zur Verstärkung des Eindrucks „urbanen Lebens" hervorgehoben werden. Die Tiefe des an sich schon länglichen Raums wird durch die Anordnung der Bereiche noch betont. Die zur Unterbrechung des Grundrisses fehlenden Wände werden durch einen Stahlkasten ersetzt, der in seiner Abstufung dabei hilft, den als Essbereich/Besprechungstisch vorgesehenen Raum abzugrenzen. Dieser Raum dient auch als Küche, deren Geschirr wiederum hinter einer großen Metallkonsole verdeckt ist. Am Ende sorgt eine Reihe violett beleuchteter Glaspaneele für ein Trennung der Schlafzimmer- und Badbereiche, ohne dabei jedoch den Wegen ihre Transparenz zu nehmen.

› Plan Plan Grundriss

Frank + Amy

Resolution: 4 Architecture
New York, United States

These premises in the center of New York occupy an entire floor of an old industrial building and were designed for a film critic and an editor. The large windows with dynamic views of the city play a key role in the division of the space. The conceptual approach to the construction enhances the industrial atmosphere and converts it into a sculptural intervention in the pre-existing space. The result is a complex, compact cube that separates the public and private areas and becomes the structural axis of the space. The use of different materials was determined by the abundant light in the loft. Different types of woods were used to create a harmonious and warm atmosphere. The pipes and ducts for the electrical installation and heating were left uncovered on the ceiling, serving as decoration and recalling the building's functional, industrial past.

Ce logement au centre de New York, occupant l'étage entier d'un vieux bâtiment industriel, a été conçu pour un critique cinématographique et un éditeur. Les grandes fenêtres avec vue panoramique sur la cité jouent un rôle clé dans la division de l'espace. L'approche conceptuelle de la construction souligne l'atmosphère industrielle de l'espace préexistant, tout en lui conférant un aspect sculptural. Il en résulte un cube compact et complexe qui sépare les zones privées et publiques et devient l'axe structural de l'espace. L'abondance de lumière dans le loft a été un critère décisif dans le choix des matériaux. L'atmosphère harmonieuse et chaude est le fruit de différentes essences de bois. Au plafond, les tuyaux et conduits de l'installation électrique et du chauffage sont apparents. Devenus éléments de décoration, ils ne sont pas sans rappeler le passé industriel de l'édifice.

Diese Wohnung wurde in einer Fabriketage eines alten Gebäudes in New York geschaffen, sie gehört einem Filmkritiker und einer Redakteurin. Das große Fenster mit einem tollen Blick auf die Stadt spielt eine Schlüsselrolle in der Raumaufteilung. Die konzeptuelle Herangehensweise an das Projekt unterstreicht die industrielle Atmosphäre und wird zu einem skulpturellen Eingriff in einen bereits existierenden Raum. Das Ergebnis ist ein komplexer und kompakter Würfel, der die öffentlichen von den privaten Bereichen trennt und zur strukturellen Achse der Räume wird. Durch die Verwendung verschiedenster Materialien erhält das Loft sehr viel Licht. Mit mehreren Holzarten wurde eine harmonische und warme Atmosphäre geschaffen. Die Rohre und Leitungen der elektrischen Installationen und der Heizung verlaufen sichtbar an der Decke. Sie dienen als Dekorationselemente und erinnern an die funktionelle und industrielle Vergangenheit des Gebäudes.

The space is organized around a cube, which distributes the space by separating the various spaces in different directions.

L'espace s'articule autour d'un cube qui le distribue en séparant diverses zones dans des directions différentes.

Um eine Würfelform herum wurden die Räume unterteilt und in verschiedene Richtungen organisiert.

› **Perspective** Perspective Perspektivzeichnung

› **Plan** Plan Grundriss

The Factory

3W London
Norwich, United Kingdom

This former factory is located in the city of Norwich in the east of England. It sits on the banks of the River Wensum, close to the local rail station, in a brownfield site that has recently been redeveloped into a residential zone. The conversion project has boxed 24 loft units onto the factory's four levels. These are the first loft dwellings to be constructed in Norwich, varying in size from 90 to 150 m². This loft has an ecological design that was envisaged to dovetail 'perfection' and modern interior spaces emphasizing brightness and spaciousness. Some of its most extraordinary features include the floor-to-ceiling windows and the barrel vaulted ceilings. Predominantly white and cream shades have been chosen to decorate the interior and enhance the role of light. The results are striking.

Cette ancienne usine située dans la ville de Norwich, à l'Est de la Grande-Bretagne, est tout proche de la station de trains. Elle se trouve dans une zone industrielle récemment rénovée et reconvertie en quartier résidentiel, au bord de la rivière Wensum. La reconversion a permis d'aménager 24 appartements type loft sur 4 étages ; les premiers à avoir été construits dans la ville. Leurs superficies varient entre 90 et 150 m². Le concept de l'appartement est écologique et a été réalisé dans le but de le marier à la perfection à des intérieurs modernes qui misent sur la luminosité et l'espace. Les fenêtres qui vont du sol au plafond et les toits qui possèdent une voûte en berceau sont mis en évidence. Le blanc prédomine dans les espaces intérieurs afin d'accentuer le rôle de la lumière, et les tons crème donnent un résultat remarquable.

Diese alte Fabrik in Norwich, im Osten Großbritanniens, liegt unweit vom Bahnhof und innerhalb eines vor kurzem restaurierten und in ein Wohngebiet verwandelten Industriegebiets am Ufer des Flusses Wensum. Durch den Umbau wurde der Bau von 24 Appartements im Loft-Stil – als erste ihrer Art in der Stadt – auf vier Etagen ermöglicht. Die 90 bis 150 m² großen Appartements wurden unter ökologischen Aspekten entworfen und passen sich an moderne Innenraumdesigns, bei denen Helligkeit und Geräumigkeit vorherrschen, perfekt an. Hervorzuheben sind die vom Boden bis zur Decke reichenden Glaswände und das Tonnengewölbe. In den Innenräumen wurden bevorzugt Weiß- und Cremetöne eingesetzt, um den Lichteinfall zu betonen, womit wirklich beachtliche Ergebnisse erzielt wurden.

Conserving certain industrial vestiges, such as the concrete beam in the living space ceiling, was one of the best interior design decisions made by the architects.

La conservation de quelques-uns des vestiges industriels, tels que la poutre en béton du plafond du salon est un des succès de la création de ces intérieurs.

Die Erhaltung einiger industrieller Überreste, wie zum Beispiel des Betonträgers im Wohnzimmer, ist ein Grund für den großen Erfolg des Innendesigns.

As the bedroom is the smallest room, a large mirror was chosen to 'double' the space.

La chambre à coucher est la pièce la plus petite, et pour cela, un grand miroir a été choisi afin de produire un effet d'espace double.

Im kleinsten Raum, dem Schlafzimmer, montierte man einen Spiegel, der den Raum optisch vergrößern sollte.

Loft in Montrouge

Jean-Pierre Lévêque
Montrouge, France

In this project, the architect Jean-Pierre Lévêque was able to take advantage of the volume and light provided by a 19th-century factory building to create a home spread over four levels with a configuration that differed from the original layout. The project set up an interplay between containers and contents, an intelligent puzzle dominated by continuity; the insertion of autonomous elements in some areas provides intimacy and the feeling of being either inside or outside. The cube shapes and straight lines flow smoothly into one another. The distribution was designed to attain a continuity that makes it possible to go up to the next level and then return below without straying from a single path. This was achieved with a specific program that designed the spaces independently of the functions that they would take on. These functions were adapted to the project afterwards, as the system made it possible to define the use that would be given to each space with geometrical precision.

Pour ce projet, l'architecte Jean-Pierre Lévêque a su tirer parti du volume et de la lumière de cette usine du XIXᵉ siècle, pour créer un logement organisé sur quatre étages, d'après un plan différent de l'original. Ce projet se base sur l'interaction entre les contenants et leur contenu. C'est un puzzle bien pensé sous le signe de la continuité. L'intégration, en certains endroits, d'éléments autonomes favorise l'intimité et la sensation de n'être ni exclu, ni enfermé. Les formes et lignes droites du cube se fondent en douceur les unes aux autres. La conception de l'organisation de l'espace s'inscrit dans la continuité, ce qui permet de passer d'un niveau à l'autre en suivant le même chemin. Ceci a été rendu possible par un programme spécifique qui concevait les espaces indépendamment de leurs fonctions. Le rôle de chaque pièce a été défini plus tard, grâce à ce système permettant d'attribuer la fonction à chaque espace avec une précision d'horloger.

Der Architekt Jean-Pierre Lévêque nutzte bei der Planung dieses Lofts die Formen und das Licht in dem Fabrikgebäude aus dem 19. Jahrhundert aus, um eine Wohnung auf vier Ebenen zu schaffen, die sich von der ursprünglichen Ausstattung unterscheidet. Das Projekt stellt eine Art Wechselspiel zwischen Behälter und Inhalt dar, ein intelligentes Puzzle, das sich durch Kontinuität auszeichnet. Durch das Einfügen unabhängiger Elemente in einige Bereiche wird Privatsphäre geschaffen und das Gefühl, sich innen oder außen zu befinden. Die geraden Formen und Linien der Würfel gehen sanft ineinander über. Durch diese Verteilung wurde eine Kontinuität erreicht, die es ermöglicht, auf demselben Weg nach oben und wieder nach unten zu gehen. Dies wurde erreicht, indem man die Räume unabhängig von ihrer Funktion gestaltete. Hier wurden die Funktionen später der Planung angepasst. Dieses System machte es möglich, die Benutzung der Räume mit geometrischer Genauigkeit zu definieren.

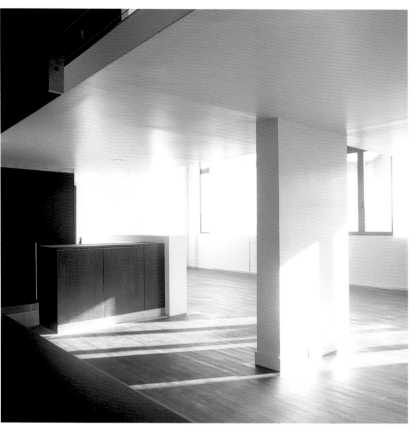

The materials used underline the general concept: the parquet, made of maçaranduba wood, helps to unify the space, while the stainless steel of the staircase lightens it.

Les matériaux employés soulignent le concept général : le parquet, en bois de macaranduba unifie l'espace, mis en valeur par la rampe en acier inoxydable de l'escalier.

Durch den gezielten Einsatz bestimmter Materialien wurde das grundlegende Konzept noch unterstrichen. Das Massaranduba-Parkett vereinheitlicht den Raum, und der Edelstahl des Handlaufs der Treppe macht ihn heller.

› **Ground floor** Rez-de-chaussée Erdgeschoss

› **Mezzanine** Mezzanine Zwischengeschoss

The various spaces were first designed independently of their functions to form an intelligent puzzle dominated by the theme of continuity.

Au départ, les différents espaces ont été conçus indépendamment de leurs fonctions pour former un puzzle astucieux, régi par l'idée de continuité.

Bei der Gestaltung der verschiedenen Räume wurde zunächst deren Funktion außer Acht gelassen. So entstand ein intelligentes Puzzle, dessen Grundlage die Kontinuität ist.

Loft on Rue Arthur Rozier

Alessandro Mosca
Paris, France

In order to take maximum advantage of the height of this old print shop in Paris, the architect Alessandro Mosca divided the space horizontally and drew up a mezzanine that is accessed by two different stretches of staircase. The configuration of the staircase, the loft's central element, leads to the unusual layout of the upper floor: to one side, the bedroom and the studio; on the other, the bathroom. This also facilitates an interesting distribution of the spaces on the ground floor. As the building's structure is very old, the mezzanine was supported by an independent structure. Moreover, it does not occupy the overall surface area but pulls back slightly to allow light to pour in from the courtyard through the windows and the skylights. The conversion uses simple, cheap and resistant materials, while the decoration establishes a contrast between the dominant pale colors on the walls and a scattering of bright red elements.

Pour optimiser la hauteur de cette ancienne imprimerie parisienne, l'architecte Alessandro Mosca a divisé l'espace horizontalement et aménagé une mezzanine accessible par deux escaliers différents. La configuration de l'escalier, élément central du loft, mène à l'étage supérieur conçu de manière inhabituelle : la chambre à coucher et le studio d'un côté, et la salle de bains de l'autre. Au rez-de-chaussée, la distribution de l'espace est, également originale. Compte tenu l'ancienneté de l'ossature de l'édifice, une structure indépendante a été installée pour soutenir la mezzanine. Toutefois, elle ne couvre pas toute la surface mais s'inscrit légèrement en retrait, permettant à la lumière de la cour de pénétrer par les fenêtres et les velux. Des matériaux bon marché et résistants ont été employés pour la restauration. Sur le plan décoratif, les couleurs pâles dominantes des murs contrastent avec les taches rouge vif de quelques éléments épars.

Um die Höhe dieser ehemaligen Druckerei in Paris zu nutzen, unterteilte der Architekt Alessandro Mosca den Raum horizontal und zog ein Zwischengeschoss ein, das über zwei verschiedene Treppenabschnitte zu erreichen ist. Die Treppe ist das zentrale Element des Lofts und führt zu dem ungewöhnlich aufgeteilten Obergeschoss. Auf einer Seite befinden sich Schlafzimmer und Studio, auf der anderen Seite das Badezimmer. Da die Gebäudestruktur sehr alt ist, wurde das Zwischengeschoss mit einer unabhängigen Struktur gestützt. Das Zwischengeschoss nimmt nicht die ganze Ebene ein, sondern ist leicht zurückversetzt, sodass Licht durch die Fenster und Oberlichter einfallen kann. Für den Umbau wurden einfache, preisgünstige und widerstandsfähige Materialien verwendet, und in der Dekoration wurde der Gegensatz zwischen den dominanten blassen Farben der Wand und einzelnen hellroten Elementen unterstrichen.

The configuration of the staircase sets up an interesting distribution of space and visually separates the areas that differentiate the kitchen and the living area.

La configuration de l'escalier crée une distribution intéressante de l'espace, instaurant une division visuelle et spatiale entre la cuisine et le salon.

Durch die Gestaltung der Treppe entstand eine interessante Raumaufteilung: Sie trennt den Küchen- und den Wohnbereich visuell voneinander ab.

› **Ground floor** Rez-de-chaussée Erdgeschoss

› **First floor** Premier étage Erstes Obergeschoss

The mezzanine does not occupy the overall surface area but pulls back slightly to allow light to pour in through the windows and the skylights.

La mezzanine n'occupe pas toute la surface mais elle est légèrement en retrait pour permettre à la lumière naturelle de pénétrer à travers les fenêtres et les velux.

Das Zwischengeschoss nimmt nicht die ganze Ebene ein, sondern ist leicht zurückgesetzt, sodass Licht durch die Fenster und Oberlichter einfallen kann.

Cortés Loft

Pepe Cortés Asociados
Barcelona, Spain

These premises in Barcelona, formerly a textile warehouse, were converted by the prestigious designer Pepe Cortés into his own home. The existing height permitted the construction of a loft that includes a terrace with a garden and a swimming pool. The large windows on the upper level allow the entire space to be flooded with natural light. Areas are marked out by sliding doors, curtains and perforated partitions, which are translucent but can provide privacy when necessary. The project brings together a great variety of materials—either recycled from the original building, such as the iron in the column and wood in part of the structure, or new elements like marble, plaster painted in bright colors, aluminum and glass. Cortés personalized the settings with artworks created by friends, souvenirs from trips, and various well-known pieces of furniture of his own design.

Pepe Cortés, designer de renom, a transformé cet ancien entrepôt de textile de Barcelone, pour y élire domicile. La hauteur du bâtiment a permis de construire un loft avec une terrasse, un jardin et une piscine. Les larges baies vitrées du niveau supérieur inondent l'espace de lumière naturelle. Portes coulissantes, rideaux et cloisons ajourés translucides délimitent les pièces, tout en assurant, si besoin est, une certaine intimité. Le projet réunit une grande diversité de matériaux – certains récupérés de l'ancien bâtiment, comme le fer dans les piliers et le bois dans certaines parties de la structure ou d'autres nouveaux éléments tels que le marbre, le plâtre peint dans des couleurs vives, l'aluminium et le verre. Pour personnaliser la construction, Cortés a ajouté des œuvres d'art créées par des amis, des souvenirs de voyage et plusieurs meubles design très connus, fruits de sa création.

Diese Räume in Barcelona liegen in einem ehemaligen Lagerhaus für Textilien, das der bekannte Designer Pepe Cortés zu seiner eigenen Wohnung umbaute. Die sehr hohen Räume erlaubten ein Loft mit angrenzender Terrasse zu schaffen, auf der sich ein Garten und ein Swimmingpool befinden. Durch die großen Fenster auf der oberen Ebene dringt reichlich Tageslicht ein. Die verschiedenen Bereiche sind durch Schiebetüren, Vorhänge und lichtdurchlässige Raumteiler mit Öffnungen abgeteilt. So kann man Privatsphäre schaffen, wenn es notwendig ist. Bei der Gestaltung wurden viele verschiedene Materialien eingesetzt, die wie das Eisen der Säulen und das Holz an Teilen der Struktur aus dem Originalgebäude stammen, oder wie der Marmor, der Gips in hellen Farben, Aluminium und Glas neu hinzugefügt wurden. Cortés dekorierte sein Zuhause sehr persönlich mit von Freunden gestalteten Kunstwerken, Reisesouvenirs und verschiedenen bekannten Möbelstücken aus seiner eigenen Kollektion.

The numerous works of art reinforce the dynamic and colorful spirit that guided the design of all of the rooms in the residence.

Les nombreuses œuvres d'art exaltent le design dynamique et haut en couleur qui caractérise toutes les pièces de la résidence.

Die zahlreichen Kunstwerke unterstreichen die dynamische und bunte Atmosphäre, die die Gestalter geschaffen haben.

› **Ground floor** Rez-de-chaussée Erdgeschoss

› **First floor** Premier étage Erstes Obergeschoss

The upper level boasts two magnificent terraces; the swimming pool and lush vegetation have turned it into an authentic urban oasis.

Le niveau supérieur se targue de deux superbes terrasses. La piscine et la végétation exubérante le métamorphosent en une véritable oasis en plein cœur de la ville.

Im Obergeschoss befinden sich zwei wundervolle Terrassen. Der Swimmingpool und eine üppige Vegetation machen diese zu einer wahren Stadtoase.

Flower District Loft

Desai/Chia Studio
New York, United States

The client of this New York loft wanted a design that would accommodate office work by day and large business events or intimate social gatherings by night. The open public areas are visually choreographed so that they can merge, compress, and expand, depending on the client's needs. Its "elasticity" allows it to expand for a large, crowded party or to contract into separate zones for the more intimate gatherings and events. A compact volume of private space contains a guest bedroom, gym, powder-room, and two bathrooms, compressing the center of the public area into the kitchen, which becomes the focal point of the loft. Translucent screen doors mounted on aluminum frames allow the passage of light from the private core to the public areas. Their pattern, inspired by the traditional Indian jali, creates a shifting pattern of translucency, depending on the direction in which the light passes through the materials.

A la requête du client, ce loft de New York, conçu pour faire office de bureau pendant la journée, sert de salle de grandes réunions d'affaires ou de réceptions sociales plus intimes, le soir. Les espaces ouverts au public, selon une mise en scène visuelle, fusionnent, se compriment et s'élargissent au gré des besoins du client. Cette « élasticité » permet de moduler l'espace : l'élargir pour une grande réception ou le diviser en petites zones séparées pour les réunions ou événements à caractère privé. Le volume d'une unité privée comprend une chambre d'invités, une salle de gymnastique, un boudoir et deux salles de bains, limitant le centre de la partie publique à la cuisine, le point de mire du loft. Des portes de verre translucide montées sur châssis d'aluminium laissent passer la lumière de la sphère privée aux zones publiques. Leurs motifs, inspirés du jali indien traditionnel, créent des jeux de lumière changeants, au gré des matériaux qu'elle traverse.

Für dieses Loft in New York wünschte sich der Kunde eine Gestaltung, die sich tagsüber für berufliche Zwecke sowie abends für Geschäftsveranstaltungen oder private Zusammenkünfte nutzen lässt. Die offenen Bereiche können visuell verändert und je nach Wunsch zusammengeschlossen, verkleinert oder vergrößert werden. Diese Flexibilität ermöglicht sowohl eine große, belebte Party als auch kleine Treffen und private Gespräche. Ein kompaktes Volumen mit Privaträumen enthält ein Gästezimmer, einen Sportraum und zwei Badezimmer. Das Zentrum des öffentlichen Bereiches bildet die Küche, die somit auch Mittelpunkt des Lofts ist. Lichtdurchlässige Türen auf Aluminiumrahmen lassen Tageslicht einfallen, das von den privaten Räumen in die öffentlich genutzten vordringt. Ihre Muster, inspiriert von dem traditionellen indischen Jali, lassen Lichtmuster entstehen, die sich verändern, wenn das Licht aus einer anderen Richtung durch das Material fällt.

The client wanted a design that would accommodate office work by day and large business events or intimate social gatherings by night.

Le client voulait un espace design qui puisse accueillir des bureaux pendant la journée et d'importantes réunions d'affaires ou de réceptions plus intimes le soir.

Der Kunde wünschte sich eine Raumgestaltung, die sowohl für die Büroarbeit tagsüber als auch für längere geschäftliche Treffen oder private Zusammenkünfte an den Abenden geeignet ist.

› Plan Plan Grundriss

The kitchen made of walnut and stainless steel becomes the focal point of the loft and takes advantage of the light coming in from the floor-to-ceiling windows.

La cuisine en noyer et acier inoxydable est le point de mire du loft. Elle bénéficie de la lumière qui arrive par les baies vitrées.

Die Küche aus Nussbaum und Edelstahl ist der Mittelpunkt des Lofts. Hier dringt direktes Licht durch das deckenhohe Fenster ein.

Translucent screen doors mounted on aluminum frames allow light to pass from the private core to the public areas.

Des paravents translucides montés sur châssis d'aluminium permettent à la lumière de passer des sphères privées aux zones publiques.

Die Türen auf Aluminiumrahmen lassen das Licht durch, das von den privaten Zimmern in die öffentlichen Räume vordringt.

The large windows and big mirrors, as well as the stone used for the surfaces, make the bathroom bright and welcoming.

Les grandes fenêtres et immenses miroirs alliés à la pierre des revêtements de surfaces agrandissent la salle de bains lumineuse et accueillante.

Die riesigen Fenster und großen Spiegel und die mit Naturstein verkleideten Wände schaffen eine helle und freundliche Atmosphäre im Badezimmer.

Rosenberg Residence

Belmont Freeman Architects
New York, United States

This residence, a multi-use project in an early-20th-century commercial building, is spread over two 1,500-sq-ft floors, converted into a living space during the 1980s. The two floors are vertically connected, with the interior renovated as an office, studio, and home for the art-loving occupant. From the outset, this special relationship between the two units played a prominent role, and the architects managed to develop a language that paradoxically joins both parts and makes them independent. On the upper floor, the home contains a living-room, a kitchen, and two bedrooms. No partitions break up the exterior wall, which lets in abundant light from the north. The lower level, with its restored, sandblasted, concrete flooring cast with zinc, serves as both office and studio. The two levels are connected by a staircase that seems to have come straight from a ship and separates the work area and the living area on the upper floor.

Cette résidence, un projet polyvalent dans un bâtiment commercial du début du XXᵉ siècle, d'une superficie au sol de 140 m², a été transformée en surface habitable dans les années 80. Les deux étages sont reliés verticalement. L'intérieur a été restauré en bureau, studio et logement pour un amoureux de l'art. Dès le départ, la relation particulière entre les deux unités a joué un rôle prépondérant, amenant les architectes à développer un langage paradoxal qui permet de les joindre tout en les gardant indépendant. Au niveau supérieur, on trouve un salon, une cuisine et deux chambres. Le mur extérieur n'est pas divisé et laisse pénétrer à flots la lumière du nord. Le niveau inférieur, au sol rénové en béton à jets de sable et zinc, sert à la fois de bureau et de studio. Les deux niveaux sont reliés par un escalier qui semble venir directement d'un bateau. Il sépare le salon du bureau à l'étage.

Diese vielseitig genutzten Räume in einem Geschäftshaus aus dem frühen 20. Jahrhundert sind 140 m² groß und wurden 1980 in Wohnräume umgestaltet. Die beiden Etagen sind vertikal miteinander verbunden und Büro, Atelier und die Wohnung des Besitzers wurden renoviert. Die besondere Beziehung zwischen den beiden Einheiten spielte von Anfang an eine wichtige Rolle, und dem Architekten gelang es, diese beiden Einheiten miteinander zu verbinden und gleichzeitig voneinander unabhängig zu gestalten. Auf der oberen Etage befinden sich das Wohnzimmer, die Küche und zwei Schlafzimmer. Die äußere Wand wird nicht unterbrochen und es strömt viel Licht von Norden ein. Das untere Stockwerk mit seinem restaurierten, sandgestrahlten Betonboden mit Zink dient sowohl als Büro als auch als Atelier. Die beiden Ebenen werden durch eine Treppe verbunden, die von einem Schiff zu stammen scheint und die den Arbeitsbereich von dem Wohnbereich trennt.

Hatchway-like stairs connect the two levels and separate the work area from the private quarters on the upper floor.

Des escaliers, faisant penser à des écoutilles, relient entre eux les deux niveaux, séparant l'espace bureau des quartiers privés à l'étage.

Treppen, die wie für Ladeluken gemacht wirken, verbinden die beiden Ebenen und trennen den Arbeits- vom Wohnbereich im Obergeschoss ab.

› **Ground floor** Rez-de-chaussée Erdgeschoss

› First floor Premier étage Erstes Obergeschoss

The furnishings in the kitchen and the bathroom were exclusively designed for the project.

Le mobilier de la cuisine et de la salle de bains a été conçu exclusivement pour ce projet.

Das Mobiliar der Küche und des Badezimmers wurde exklusiv für diese Räume entworfen.

Loft in Amsterdam

Dick van Gameren/
De Architectengroep
Amsterdam, The Netherlands

This fully restored loft space preserved its wooden beams and large façade windows by incorporating a central module that distributes the day and night areas. The central unit, whose walls stop short of the ceiling to maintain spatial fluidity, incorporates a seamless series of cupboards and drawers, one of which pulls into a dining table. On the façade side, the kitchen installations take advantage of the light and views. A sliding, translucent glass door leads on to the bedroom and beyond. The opposite side contains room for storage and also leads to the bedroom. It can be closed off by a series of sliding panels that hang from a railing. The bathroom is contained within the unit; its opaque glass panel above the bathtub acts as the kitchen wall on the other side. An opening was maintained above the bathroom to avoid humidity and to allow light to enter the space.

Ce loft entièrement restauré a gardé ses poutres de bois et ses grandes baies vitrées d'origine en intégrant un module central autour duquel s'articulent les parties jour et les parties nuits. Les murs de cet axe central ne montent pas jusqu'au plafond pour conserver la fluidité de l'espace. Toute une série de placards et tiroirs à bords lisses y sont encastrés, et l'un d'eux se transforme en table. Du côté de la façade, la cuisine bénéficie de la lumière et de la vue. Une cloison de verre translucide coulissante s'ouvre sur la chambre et au-delà, sur un espace rangement qui communique aussi avec elle. Cette partie peut être masquée par une série de cloisons coulissantes suspendues à un rail. Une salle de bains est également intégrée au module. Une cloison de verre opaque à côté de la baignoire fait aussi office de mur pour la cuisine située de l'autre côté. Au-dessus de la baignoire, une ouverture contre l'humidité permet à la lumière de pénétrer dans l'espace.

In diesem renovierten Loft blieben die Holzbalken und die großen Fenster erhalten, und es wurde ein zentrales Modul eingebaut, das die Bereiche für den Tag und die Nacht unterteilt. Diese zentrale Einheit, deren Wände nicht bis zur Decke reichen, um den Raum nicht zu unterbrechen, enthält eine nahtlose Reihe von Schränken und Schubladen, von denen eine zum Esstisch wird. Die Arbeitsseite der Küche liegt bei den Fenstern, hell und mit Ausblick. Eine lichtdurchlässige Schiebetür aus Glas führt zum Schlafzimmer und weiter. Auf der anderen Seite gibt es einen Lagerraum und man gelangt ebenfalls zum Schlafzimmer. Dieses kann durch eine Reihe von gleitenden Paneelen verschlossen werden. Das Badezimmer befindet sich ebenfalls in dieser Einheit, das undurchsichtige Glaspaneel über der Badewanne ist gleichzeitig die Küchenwand. Eine Öffnung an der Kopfseite des Badezimmers sorgt für Licht und verhindert die Bildung von Feuchtigkeit.

The inserted central module distribute the day and night areas while maintaining the spatial fluidity of the whole space.

Le module central intégré distribue les aires de jour et de nuit tout en conservant la fluidité spatiale de l'espace entier.

Das eingefügte zentrale Modul unterteilt die Bereiche in Zonen für tagsüber und nachts, ohne dabei die Kontinuität des gesamten Raumes zu unterbrechen.

› Plan Plan Grundriss

The module contains storage space and can be closed off by a series of sliding panels that hang from a railing.

Le module offre un espace de rangement qui peut être fermé par une série de cloisons coulissantes suspendes à un rail.

In dem Modul ist Stauraum vorhanden, und es kann mit einer Reihe von gleitenden Paneelen auf Schienen abgeschlossen werden.

An opening was maintained above the bathroom to avoid humidity and to allow light to enter the space.

L'ouverture maintenue au-dessus de la salle de bains permet d'éliminer l'humidité et d'inonder l'espace de lumière.

Eine Öffnung über dem Badezimmer sorgt für Licht und verhindert die Bildung von Feuchtigkeit.

Manuel Ocaña del Valle
Madrid, Spain

Loft in an Attic

This loft in a 150-year-old building in Madrid was transformed from a small space unsuitable for domestic purposes to a modern residence. To expand the usable floor space, the architect took advantage of the high ceilings and, in the tallest part of the space, under the sloping roof, he divided the area into two levels. The utmost care was taken to optimize the space, and the result is a playful exploration of the concept of a home that avoids traditional, rigid models and emphasizes functional flexibility. When the residents want to eat, the entire loft becomes a dining-room; when they want to sit down, the entire space turns into a living-room; and when they want to sleep, the entire apartment is a bedroom. Technical rigor and constructional precision were the essential tools for the successful completion of the project.

Situé dans un édifice madrilène vieux de 150 ans, ce loft, petit espace inadapté aux besoins d'une famille, a été restructuré en une résidence moderne. Pour augmenter l'espace utilitaire au sol, l'architecte a tiré parti de la hauteur de plafond : sous le toit en pente et au plus haut point, il a divisé l'espace en deux parties. L'espace a donc été optimalisé au maximum. Le résultat final est une maison conçue dans une approche ludique, loin des modèles traditionnels et rigides, exaltant ainsi la flexibilité fonctionnelle. A l'heure des repas, tout le loft devient salle à manger ; lorsque les occupants veulent s'asseoir, l'espace entier se métamorphose en salon et à l'heure du coucher, l'ensemble de l'appartement se transforme en chambre à coucher. La réussite de ce projet repose sur la rigueur technique et la précision de la construction.

Dieses Loft in einem 150 Jahre alten Gebäude in Madrid wurde von einem unbewohnbaren, kleinen Raum in eine moderne Wohnung umgebaut. Um mehr Platz zu schaffen, nutzte der Architekt die hohen Decken und zog im höchsten Teil unter dem geneigten Dach eine zweite Ebene ein. Ziel war es, den Raum optimal auszunutzen. So entstand die verspielte Interpretation einer Wohnung, in der traditionelle und steife Modelle vermieden und eine funktionelle Vielseitigkeit betont werden. Wenn die Bewohner essen möchten, wird das ganze Loft zum Esszimmer, möchten sie sich hinsetzen, wird alles zum Wohnzimmer, und möchten sie schlafen, ist die ganze Wohnung das Schlafzimmer. Das wurde mit sehr präzise eingesetzten Bautechniken erreicht.

The ingenious design has created a wooden terrace extending into the interior, producing a platform that can be used for sitting outdoors.

Fruit d'un design ingénieux, la terrasse extérieure se prolonge vers l'intérieur, créant une plate-forme qui peut être utilisée pour s'asseoir dehors.

Teil der interessanten Gestaltung ist eine Terrasse aus Holz, die sich nach innen erstreckt und eine Plattform bildet, auf der man draußen sitzen kann.

› **Ground floor** Rez-de-chaussée Erdgeschoss

› **First floor** Premier étage Erstes Obergeschoss

› Longitudinal sections   Sections longitudinales   Längsschnitte

House in Fukaya

Waro Kishi +
K. Associates/Architects
Fukaya, Japan

This house is located in a site often described as a city suburb, due to its proximity to central Tokyo. As for the location, the architect Waro Kishi chose a closed configuration, while keeping an open interior space. The house has a rectangular layout, with the southern part containing the private elements, the garage and bedrooms, spread over two levels. The northern part, which is a half-level higher, contains the living and dining areas. A courtyard with a pool is located in the center of the building, connecting the southern and northern parts while also functioning as an exterior living-room. By placing the horizontal stress on the exterior wall structure, the glass can be attached directly to two 4-inch posts, so that they stand free from both the sash windows and the wall structure. Factory materials and the visibility of the structural details give the building a real authentic character.

Cette maison se situe dans un site souvent décrit comme les faubourgs de la cité, pour sa proximité du centre de Tokyo. L'architecte Waro Kishi a choisi de créer un ensemble fermé tout en gardant un espace intérieur ouvert. La maison est de conception rectangulaire, avec au sud les parties privées, le garage et les chambres réparties sur deux niveaux. La partie nord, constituée d'un demi-étage, englobe le salon et la salle à manger. La cour dotée d'une piscine est située au centre de l'édifice. Trait d'union entre les parties sud et nord, elle fait office de salon extérieur. La tension horizontale étant placée sur l'ossature des murs extérieurs, le verre peut être directement fixé à deux tenants de 10 cm, ce qui les rend indépendants des deux fenêtres à guillotine et de l'ossature murale. Des matériaux d'usine et les détails apparents de la structure confèrent à l'édifice toute son authenticité.

Dieses Haus befindet sich in einer Gegend, die oft als Vorstadt bezeichnet wird, da sie so nah am Zentrum Tokios liegt. Aufgrund des Standortes wählte der Architekt Waro Kishi eine geschlossene Konfiguration, das Innere wurde jedoch offen gestaltet. Das Haus hat einen rechteckigen Grundriss. Im südlichen Teil befinden sich auf zwei Ebenen die privaten Räume, die Garage und die Schlafzimmer. Im nördlichen Teil, eine halbe Ebene höher, liegen Wohn- und Essbereich. Im Zentrum des Gebäudes befindet sich ein Hof mit einem Becken, der den südlichen und nördlichen Teil miteinander verbindet und gleichzeitig als Wohnzimmer im Freien dient. Die horizontale Belastung liegt auf der äußeren Wandstruktur, sodass das Glas direkt an den 10 cm dicken Pfählen angebracht werden kann und diese weder die Schiebefenster noch die Wandstruktur berühren. Das Gebäude wirkt durch den Einsatz von industriellen Materialien und den sichtbaren Strukturdetails sehr authentisch.

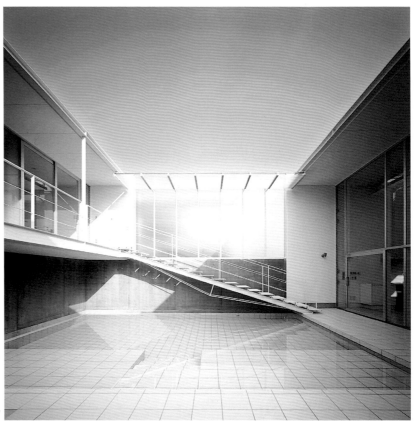

Full-height windows fill the rooms with natural light during the day and the white furniture accentuates the brightness of the space.

Des fenêtres tout en hauteur inondent les pièces de lumière du jour. Le mobilier blanc accentue l'impression d'espace.

Durch die deckenhohen Fenster fällt reichlich Tageslicht in die Räume und die weißen Möbel unterstreichen diese Helligkeit noch.

Industrial materials were used as an answer to the bleak surroundings, and the structural details are left exposed.

L'emploi de matériaux industriels contraste avec la tristesse de l'environnement. Les détails de la structure sont parfaitement mis en relief.

Als Antwort auf die etwas triste Umgebung wurden industrielle Materialien eingesetzt und die strukturellen Details nicht verborgen.

A pool has been inserted in the center of the courtyard to connect the southern and northern parts of the building.

Une piscine est intégrée au centre de l'atrium, tel un trait d'union entre les parties sud et nord du bâtiment.

Ein Becken mitten im Hof verbindet die südlichen mit den nördlichen Gebäudeteilen.

David Adjaye/
Adjaye Associates
London, United Kingdom

Dirty House

The architect David Adjave, a graduate of the London's Royal College of Art who has worked with Eduardo Souto de Moura and David Chipperfield, is known as an architect with the vision of an artist. This project involved rebuilding a warehouse to create both a studio and a home. In order to begin with an open space, the structure had to be removed by building additional support into the interior walls of the studio spaces and thus taking the load off the residential floor. The main living zone occupies the ground-floor area, while the smaller spaces—the kitchen, bathroom, bedroom, and terraces facing south and west—are located around it. The centralized nature of this arrangement is given further emphasis by a skylight in the middle and the cantilevered roof. The skylight provides a level of natural light similar to that outside.

David Adjave, architecte diplômé du London's Royal College of Art, qui a travaillé avec Eduardo Souto de Moura et David Chipperfield, à la réputation d'être un architecte qui voit les choses avec un œil d'artiste. Ce projet englobait la reconstruction d'un entrepôt en vue d'y créer un studio et une résidence. Pour ouvrir l'espace, il a fallu modifier la structure existante en insérant des supports supplémentaires dans les murs intérieurs du studio, soulageant ainsi le sol de la partie résidentielle. L'espace de vie principal occupe le rez-de-chaussée, alors que les autres cuisine, salle de bains, chambre à coucher et terrasses face au sud et à l'ouest s'articulent tout autour. Le caractère central de cette organisation est rehaussé par le puits de lumière au milieu et par le toit en encorbellement.

Der Architekt David Adjave, ausgebildet auf dem Royal College of Art in London, hat bereits mit Eduardo Souto de Moura und David Chipperfield zusammengearbeitet. Er genießt einen guten Ruf als Architekt, der außerdem den Blick eines Künstlers hat. Dieses Projekt umfasst den Umbau eines Lagerhauses zu einem Atelier und einer Wohnung. Zunächst wurden die Innenwände des Raumes, in dem das Atelier entstehen sollte, verstärkt, damit man Strukturelemente entfernen und Platz gewinnen konnte. So wurde der Boden der Wohnbereiche entlastet. Die wichtigsten Wohnräume liegen im Erdgeschoss, umgeben von den kleineren Räumen wie Küche, Bad, Schlafzimmer und den Terrassen nach Süden und Westen. Ein Oberlicht und das freitragende Dach unterstreichen die zentralisierte Gestaltung, und durch das Dachfenster wird der Raum taghell.

› **Ground floor** Rez-de-chaussée Erdgeschoss

› **First floor** Premier étage Erstes Obergeschoss

The centralized layout is given further emphasis by a skylight in the middle of the cantilevered roof.

La conception centrale est accentuée par le velux installé au cœur du toit en cantilever.

Ein Oberlicht inmitten des freitragenden Dachs unterstreicht die zentralisierte Gestaltung.

Crepain Residence

Crepain Architects
Antwerp, Belgium

This project entailed the refurbishment of an industrial park in the center of Antwerp, Belgium. The architect converted an old warehouse into a living space and office for his own use. The residence combines domestic uses and the functions of a large exhibition space for an art collection. The main aims of the design were to restore the original building and respect its elements, and the success of this approach is evidenced by the effective preservation of the barrel roofs and the reopening of windows that had been boarded over. The home's living quarters are located on the top level, arranged around the splendid west-facing terrace. The kitchen and bathrooms are close to the elevator shaft, where all the electrical installations are assembled. Concrete was used for the remodeling throughout the residence, but was treated in different ways according to its function. The terrace, for example, was covered with aluminum and dark wood.

Ce projet a pour tâche de restaurer un parc industriel au centre d'Anvers, en Belgique. L'architecte a converti un ancien entrepôt en logement et bureau pour son usage personnel. La résidence réunit les services domestiques et les fonctions d'un vaste espace d'exposition pour une collection d'art. L'objectif principal du design consistait à restaurer le bâtiment d'origine et à en respecter les éléments. La conservation des toits en berceau et la réouverture des fenêtres murées reflètent la réussite de l'initiative. Les pièces à vivre se trouvent tout en haut, agencées autour d'une magnifique terrasse, face à l'est. La cuisine et les salles de bains sont proches de la cage de l'ascenseur où se trouve le système électrique. Le béton a été utilisé pour le remodelage de toute la résidence et traité différemment selon sa fonction : recouvert d'aluminium sur la terrasse, ou ailleurs, plaqué de bois sombre pour obtenir un fini plus chaleureux.

Dieses Projekt war Teil der Sanierung der Industrieanlagen im Zentrum von Antwerpen, Belgien. Der Architekt baute ein altes Warenhaus für sich selbst zu Wohnung und Studio um. Hier wird gewohnt, aber es gibt auch einen großen Ausstellungsraum für Kunstwerke. Beim Umbau sollte vor allem das Originalgebäude restauriert und seine Elemente respektiert werden, was den Planern ausgezeichnet gelang. Das Dach blieb sehr gut erhalten, und alle geschlossenen Fensteröffnungen wurden wieder geöffnet. Die Wohnräume im Obergeschoss umgeben eine wundervolle, nach Westen ausgerichtete Terrasse. Die Küche und das Badezimmer liegen in der Nähe des Fahrstuhlschachtes, in dem alle elektrischen Installationen untergebracht sind. In allen Räumen verwendete man Beton, der aber je nach Funktion anders behandelt wurde. Auf der Terrasse wurde er mit Aluminium verkleidet und dort, wo ein wärmeres Material vonnöten war, mit dunklem Holz.

› Cross section Section transversale Querschnitt

› Longitudinal section Section longitudinale Längsschnitt

Christophe Ponceau
Paris, France

Loft on Rue Volta

The architect Christophe Ponceau managed to convert these premises into a comfortable home, despite two major restrictions: on the one hand, the strong, reticulated, concrete structure that could not be modified in any way and, on the other, a ceiling that was 6 ft high at the beams and only 8 ft high in the rest of the living space. The existing floor of granite slabs was totally removed and a fine layer of white cement with earth-colored flecks poured over the entire floor to enhance the feeling of spaciousness. In order to avoid breaking the stream of natural light coming in from outside, a window was placed in the partition between the living-room and the studio. In this way, a visual relationship was also established between the rooms. Nearly all of the furniture was specially designed by the architect himself, creating a warm atmosphere.

L'architecte Christophe Ponceau a réussi à transformer ce bâtiment en un logement confortable, malgré deux contraintes majeures : d'un côté la structure massive et réticulée en béton, impossible à modifier, et de l'autre un plafond de deux mètres de haut au niveau des poutres pour deux mètres et demi dans le reste de l'espace de vie. Pour rehausser la sensation d'espace, le sol pavé en granit préexistant a été éliminé et remplacé par une fine couche de ciment blanc, ponctué de couleur terre. Afin de laisser passer la lumière naturelle venant de l'extérieur, une fenêtre a été installée dans la cloison séparant le salon du studio, ce qui crée un lien visuel entre les pièces. Tous les meubles ou presque, œuvres de l'architecte lui-même, créent une atmosphère chaleureuse.

Dem Architekten Christophe Ponceau gelang es, ein komfortables Heim zu schaffen, obwohl es dabei zwei Hindernisse gab. Zum einen die massive Stahlbetonstruktur, die nicht verändert werden konnte, und zum anderen die Decke, die an den Tragbalken nur 2 m, im übrigen Wohnbereich jedoch 2,50 m hoch war. Der bereits vorhandene Boden aus Granitplatten wurde vollständig entfernt und eine Schicht weißen Zements mit erdfarbenen Flecken auf den gesamten Fußboden aufgetragen, um das Gefühl von Weite zu verstärken. Ein Fenster in der Trennwand zwischen Wohnzimmer und Studio lässt das Tageslicht durch jeden dieser Räume strömen und schafft so eine visuelle Beziehung zwischen den beiden Räumen. Der Architekt entwarf zudem fast alle Möbel, die eine sehr warme Atmosphäre schaffen.

The furniture design breaks up the pre-existing rigid structural system. Mobile modules, sliding doors and movable shelves make it possible to easily change the appearance of the residence.

Le design du mobilier rompt avec la rigidité du système structurel préexistant. Modules mobiles, portes coulissantes et étagères amovibles permettent de modifier facilement l'aspect de la résidence.

Durch die Gestaltung der Möbel wird das bereits vorhandene steife Struktursystem unterbrochen. Bewegliche Module, Schiebetüren und bewegliche Regale machen es möglich, das Aussehen der Räume zu verändern.

› **Section** Section Schnitt

› **Plan** Plan Grundriss

Blue ceramic tiles are combined with white bathroom elements to create a cool but welcoming setting.

Les céramiques bleues conjuguées aux éléments blancs de la salle de bains créent une ambiance de fraîcheur accueillante.

Die blauen Keramikkacheln in Kombination mit den weißen Badezimmerelementen schaffen eine kühle, aber dennoch einladende Atmosphäre.

Flinders Lane

Staughton Architects
Melbourne, Australia

This former industrial space is defined by two main elements. The first is a multifunctional, free-standing wood-framed unit that encloses the sleeping area, provides storage space, serves as an auxiliary dining room, includes bookshelves, and is a sculptural element in itself. The second element is the set of patterns sandblasted into the original cement floor. The premises' industrial character was preserved by retaining features such as the original ventilation ducts, wrought-iron piping, and concrete floors. The bedroom unit is independent, touching neither the ceiling nor the lateral walls, and could easily be mistaken for a piece of furniture. While the wood and polycarbonate unit separates the space into bedroom and living room, it also delimits the kitchen and leads on to the narrow entrance of the bedroom and bathroom.

Deux éléments essentiels caractérisent cet ancien bâtiment industriel. Le premier, une unité dotée d'une ossature de bois indépendante et polyvalente, accueille un dortoir et un espace de rangement qui peut servir de salle à manger annexe. Elle abrite des étagères de livres et ressemble à une sculpture. Le deuxième élément se définit par une série de motifs imprimés au jet de sable dans le sol en ciment. Le caractère industriel du site a été conservé en gardant certains éléments, telles les gaines de ventilation d'origine, les conduites en fer forgé et les sols en béton. La chambre à coucher est une unité indépendante, ne touchant ni le plafond ni les murs latéraux, et pourrait être facilement prise pour un meuble. Une unité en bois et polycarbonate scinde l'espace en chambre à coucher et salon, et délimite aussi la cuisine. Elle mène également vers l'entrée étroite de la chambre à coucher et de la salle de bains.

Diese ehemalige Fabriketage zeichnet sich durch zwei Hauptelemente aus. Zum einen ist da die multifunktionelle freistehende Einheit mit Holzrahmen um die Schlafzimmer, in der es auch Lagerplatz und Bücherregale gibt und die als behelfsmäßiges Esszimmer dient. Sie ist in sich selbst schon ein skulpturelles Element. Das zweite Element sind die sandgeblasenen Muster auf dem originalen Zementboden. Der industrielle Charakter des Gebäudes blieb erhalten, indem Elemente wie die einstigen Belüftungskanäle, Rohre aus gehämmerten Eisen und Betonböden gezeigt werden. Die Schlafzimmereinheit ist unabhängig und berührt weder die Decke noch die Seitenwände. Man könnte sie leicht für ein Möbelstück halten. Die Einheit aus Holz und Polycarbonat trennt den Schlaf- vom Wohnbereich und begrenzt zudem die Küche; sie führt zu dem engen Zugang zum Schlafzimmer und Bad.

The wood-framed, polycarbonate unit serves as a partition wall and allows light to flow through the whole area.

L'unité en polycarbonate, encadrée de bois, sert de cloison et permet à la lumière d'inonder toute la surface.

Die holzgerahmte Einheit aus Polycarbonat dient als Trennwand und lässt überall Licht durch.

› **Plan** Plan Schnitt

Residence in Toronto

Cecconi Simone
Toronto, Canada

This loft, located in an old industrial neighborhood, was originally divided into two but these have been fused to form a single cohesive space. The designers' aim was to create a space in which the original structure and the intervention's elements would complement each other. The old truss system was preserved and the floors and columns were newly installed to recover the original color and texture and to create a rustic effect. The housing was constructed using as base units some storage cabinets found in an old factory, some enormous refrigerator doors, and some recycled pieces from a cafeteria. To match these, the architects Cecconi Simone designed a kitchen counter, a bed with incorporated lighting, and a piece of furniture for the office. The windows were left untouched, since their large dimensions offered extraordinary ventilation and outstanding views of the city.

Ce loft, situé dans un ancien quartier industriel, était à l'origine scindé en deux parties, réunies désormais pour ne former qu'un seul espace. L'idée du designer était de créer un univers où la structure originale et les éléments nouveaux seraient complémentaires. Il a gardé l'ancienne ossature et rénové les sols et les colonnes en leur donnant la couleur et la texture initiales pour créer un effet rustique. L'habitation a été construite en utilisant des armoires de rangement trouvées dans l'usine, d'énormes réfrigérateurs et des objets recyclés de cafétéria. Pour les intégrer tous, les architectes Cecconi Simone, ont dessiné le bar de la cuisine, un lit avec éclairage intégré et un meuble de bureau. Les fenêtres sont d'origine ; leur taille imposante assure une excellente ventilation et offre une superbe vue sur la ville.

Dieses Loft in einem alten Industrieviertel war einst in zwei Wohnungen unterteilt, aber es wurde zu einer zusammenhängenden Einheit umgebaut. Der Gestalter wollte innerhalb der Originalstruktur einen Raum schaffen, in dem die einzelnen, neu eingeführten Elemente einander ergänzen. Das alte Hängewerk blieb erhalten, und die Fußböden und Säulen wurden neu konstruiert, um die ehemalige Farbe und Textur wieder herzustellen und eine rustikale Wirkung zu erzielen. Die Wohnung wurde mit einigen Grundeinheiten wie Lagerschränken aus einer alten Fabrik, riesigen Kühlschranktüren und einigen recycelten Stücken aus einer Cafeteria konstruiert. Passend zu diesem Stil entwarfen die Architekten Cecconi Simone eine Küchentheke, ein Bett mit integriertem Licht und ein Möbel für das Büro. Die Fenster blieben unverändert, da sie aufgrund ihrer Größe für eine ausgezeichnete Belüftung und einen wundervollen Blick über die Stadt sorgen.

The drapes, hanging from rods in the ceiling, can be moved to change the home's configuration or even arranged to create a separate room.

Les tentures, suspendues au plafond par des cordes, peuvent être déplacées pour moduler l'espace ou même créer une pièce séparée.

Die Vorhänge sind an Stangen an der Decke aufgehängt, sodass die Aufteilung verändert werden kann. Sie können sogar so arrangiert werden, dass separate Räume entstehen.

› **Plan** Plan Schnitt

Loft in Sant Joan Despí

Agustí Costa
Sant Joan Despí, Spain

When the architect Agustí Costa set about refurbishing this studio under the roof of a detached house, he was confronted with a mixture of rustic furniture and disconnected structural elements that added up to a somewhat forbidding atmosphere. His project envisaged the creation of a living room that could be transformed into a bedroom and a work area suitable for all of the members of the family. Furthermore, the single space needed to provide sufficient privacy and isolation for different activities to be undertaken at the same time; to do this, a curved, false ceiling was installed, with openings at certain strategic points. All of the furnishings were painted the same grayish color, except for the red wall face that conceals the back of the chest of drawers, thus allowing it to assume more prominence. The lighting was integrated into the elements that structure the space.

Lorsque l'architecte Agustí Costa a entrepris la rénovation de ce studio sous les combles d'une maison individuelle, il a trouvé un mélange de meubles anciens et d'éléments structuraux dégageant une atmosphère légèrement austère. À partir de cela, il a conçu un salon modulable en chambre à coucher et une aire de travail convenant à tous les membres de la famille. Comme cet espace unique pouvait accueillir simultanément diverses activités, il était impératif de créer une certaine intimité et d'instaurer un système d'isolation. À cet effet, l'architecte a dessiné un faux plafond incurvé, doté d'ouvertures à certains points stratégiques. L'ensemble de l'ameublement se décline en gris, à l'exception d'un pan de mur rouge abritant une commode ainsi mise en valeur. L'éclairage est inséré dans les éléments structurant l'espace.

Als der Architekt Agustí Costa mit der Renovierung seines Studios im Dachgeschoss eines freistehenden Hauses begann, wurde er mit einer Mischung aus rustikalen Möbeln und unzusammenhängenden strukturellen Elementen konfrontiert, die eine nicht besonders angenehme Atmosphäre hatten entstehen lassen. Es sollte ein Wohnzimmer geschaffen werden, das in ein Schlafzimmer verwandelt werden kann sowie in einen Arbeitsbereich für alle Familienmitglieder. Dieser einzige Raum sollte aber gleichzeitig genug Privatsphäre und separate Bereiche bieten, dass verschiedene Aktivitäten zur selben Zeit stattfinden konnten. Deshalb wurde eine gebogene, zweite Decke mit strategischen Öffnungen an bestimmten Stellen installiert. Das gesamte Mobiliar wurde in der gleichen grauen Farbe gestrichen. Nur die Wand, die die Hinterwand der Kommode verbirgt, ist rot und fällt dadurch ins Auge. Die Beleuchtung ist in die Strukturelemente integriert.

All of the construction details are well thought out and the design approach is unified. The result is a coherent atmosphere that affords a space where multiple activities may be carried out.

Tous les détails de la construction sont bien conçus, sous le sceau d'un design unifié. Il en résulte une atmosphère harmonieuse, dans un espace aux fonctions multiples.

Alle Konstruktionsdetails sind gut durchdacht, sodass der Gesamteindruck sehr einheitlich ist. Eine kohärente Wohnatmosphäre, die vielen Zwecken dient.

› **Cross section** Section transversale Querschnitt

› **Plan** Plan Grundriss

House and Garage

A-cero
A Coruña, Spain

This former warehouse was transformed into a single, two-story space with minimalist lines and strong colors. Different floor levels distribute the basic functions of the loft. The lower level contains the living and dining areas. The next level, distinguished by a taller ceiling, houses an integrated kitchen that can be closed off by a sliding opaque glass panel. The top level is accessed by a floating staircase that passes alongside a glass structure containing the main bathroom. The decorative surprise arrives in the living area, where the family car appears behind a glass wall that gives on to the garage. In addition to transforming an industrial space into an innovative dwelling, the purpose of this project was to explore the social significance of the automobile as a functional and aesthetic element in the home. Glass acts as a crucial component of this concept and design.

Cet ancien entrepôt a été réhabilité en un logement individuel à deux étages, aux lignes minimalistes ponctuées de couleurs vives. Les fonctions essentielles du loft sont réparties selon un système de différence de niveaux. Le niveau inférieur abrite le salon et la salle à manger. Au niveau suivant, défini par un plafond plus élevé, se trouve une cuisine intégrée qui peut disparaître derrière un panneau de verre opaque coulissant. L'accès au plus haut niveau s'effectue par un escalier flottant qui longe une structure en verre hébergeant la salle de bains principale. L'effet de surprise, côté décoration intérieure, est à son comble lorsque l'on entre dans la pièce à vivre où la voiture de famille apparaît derrière une cloison en verre, en guise de garage. Dans ce projet, qui consistait à transformer un espace industriel en une résidence originale, s'ajoute l'étude de l'impact social de l'automobile. Ici, le verre joue un rôle déterminant dans la conception et le design.

Diese ehemalige Lagerhalle wurde zu einem zweistöckigen Raum mit minimalistischen Linien und starken Farben umgestaltet. Die Grundfunktionen des Wohnens verteilen sich auf verschiedene Ebenen. Auf der unteren Ebene befinden sich die Wohn- und Essbereiche. Auf der nächsten Ebene mit sehr hoher Decke liegt die integrierte Küche, die durch eine Schiebetür mit opaker Glasplatte geschlossen werden kann. Die oberste Etage erreicht man über eine hängende Treppe entlang der Glasstruktur, in der sich das Hauptbadezimmer befindet. Eine überraschende Dekoration findet man im Wohnbereich. Von dort aus sieht man durch eine Glaswand das Auto in der Garage. In diesem Projekt wollte man auch die soziale Bedeutung des Autos als ein funktionelles und ästhetisches Element in einem Haus zeigen. Glas ist die wichtigste Komponente bei diesem Konzept und Design.

Materials like the red rubber floor in the living room define the boundaries between the different areas.

Des matériaux, tel que le linoléum rouge sur le sol du salon, délimitent les différents espaces.

Materialien wie der rote Kautschukbelag des Fußbodens im Wohnzimmer definieren die Grenzen zwischen den verschiedenen Bereichen.

› Plan Plan Grundriss

› Sections Sections Schnitte

On the upper level, the floor was fitted out with natural coconut fiber, which adds warmth to the private space.

Le sol du niveau supérieur est revêtu de fibre naturelle de coco, conférant aux sphères privées une note chaude.

Auf der oberen Etage ist der Fußboden mit natürlicher Kokosfaser belegt, was die privaten Räume sehr warm und einladend wirken lässt.

Davol Loft

Moneo Brock Studio
New York, United States

Located in a former warehouse in downtown Manhattan's old industrial area, this project began with an empty rectangular box, characterized by the typical attributes of a loft: columns down the center, enormous windows, and a high ceiling. This distinctive spatial configuration presented a challenge if living space and a fully operational work area were to be integrated. The clients, two journalists, needed separate bedrooms with adjacent bathrooms, a kitchen, a small storage area, a large, open living-room, and a flexible work area for each of them. The service areas were placed against the windowless north and south walls but not totally separated from the rest of the loft visually, as if they were modules inserted into a container. Their walls do not reach the ceiling and iridescent materials are used to create magnificent reflective patterns that accentuate the lightness of the components.

Situé dans un vieil entrepôt de l'ancienne zone industrielle du centre de Manhattan, ce projet a commencé par une boîte rectangulaire vide, dotée des caractéristiques propres au loft : colonnes au centre, immenses fenêtres et plafond très haut. Cette configuration spatiale singulière présentait un véritable défi quant à l'intégration d'un espace salon et d'une aire de travail parfaitement opérationnelle. Les clients, deux journalistes, voulaient deux chambres séparées dotées de salles de bains contiguës, une cuisine, une petite zone de rangement, un vaste salon ouvert et une aire de travail modulable pour chacun des deux. Les zones de services ont été placées contre les murs nord et sud dépourvus de fenêtres. Mais elles ne sont pas entièrement séparées du loft sur le plan visuel, tels des modules intégrés à un container. Les murs ne montent pas jusqu'au plafond et des matériaux chatoyants créent de magnifiques motifs qui miroitent et soulignent la légèreté des éléments.

Dieses Loft in einer ehemaligen Lagerhalle im Industriegebiet von Downtown Manhattan war zunächst ein leerer, rechteckiger Kasten mit den typischen Kennzeichen einer Fabriketage: Säulen in der Mitte, riesige Fenster und eine hohe Decke. Der Umbau stellte eine Herausforderung dar, da man ein Wohnzimmer und einen voll funktionierenden Arbeitsbereich integrieren wollte. Die Kunden, zwei Journalisten, benötigten zwei getrennte Schlafzimmer mit jeweils einem anliegenden Badezimmer, eine Küche, einen kleinen Lagerraum, ein offenes Wohnzimmer und zwei flexible Arbeitsbereiche. Küche und Bad befinden sich an den fensterlosen Nord- und Südwänden, sind aber wie Module in einem Container visuell nicht vollständig vom Rest des Lofts abgetrennt. Die Wände dieser Räume reichen nicht bis zur Decke. Durch schillernde Materialien entstehen wundervolle Lichtmuster, die die Leichtigkeit und Farbigkeit der eingesetzten Elemente unterstreichen.

The finishing produces a pattern of colors, reflections, and transparencies. The extraordinary impact of this setting is the result of intense experimentation with the materials.

La finition offre une riche gamme de couleurs, de reflets et de transparences. L'impact extraordinaire de cet agencement résulte d'une étude intense des matériaux.

Durch die Verwendung der Oberflächenmaterialien entstehen Muster aus Farben, Reflexen und Transparenzen. Die außerordentliche Wirkung dieser Wohnumgebung entstand durch ein intensives Experimentieren mit den Materialien.

› Reflected ceiling plan Plan de plancher haut Deckenuntersicht

› Ground floor Rez-de-chaussée Erdgeschoss

› **Section** Section Schnitt

This large, multi-use space must meet certain acoustic requirements because the clients often use it to rehearse.

Ce vaste espace polyvalent, souvent utilisé par les clients pour répéter, doit donc remplir certaines conditions au niveau de l'acoustique.

Dieser große, multifunktionale Raum musste bestimme akustische Voraussetzungen erfüllen, da die Kunden ihn oft als Proberaum benutzen.

Some of the partitions are mobile, making it easy to redistribute the space inside the apartment. The panels' translucency sets up distinctive spatial relationships and avoids any permanent compartmentalization.

Certaines cloisons sont mobiles, ce qui permet de moduler facilement l'appartement. En évitant un cloisonnement permanent, la translucidité des panneaux crée une relation spatiale différente.

Manche der Raumteiler sind beweglich, sodass die Aufteilung der Räume sehr variabel ist. Durch die Lichtdurchlässigkeit der Paneele entstehen charakteristische räumliche Beziehungen, und eine permanente Aufteilung wird vermieden.

The walls of the bathrooms do not reach the ceiling and iridescent materials are used, creating magnificent reflecting patterns that accentuate the components' lightness and colorfulness.

Les murs de la salle de bains n'atteignent pas le plafond et les matériaux chatoyants utilisés créent des motifs et des reflets magnifiques qui rehaussent la légèreté des éléments hauts en couleur.

Die Wände des Badezimmers reichen nicht bis zur Decke. Durch schillernde Materialien entstehen wundervolle Lichtmuster, die die Leichtigkeit und Farbigkeit der eingesetzten Elemente unterstreichen.

Tank Modules

Morton Loft LOT/EK
New York, United States

Located in what was previously the fourth floor of a parking lot in New York´s West Village, this is an excellent example of a project in which the term "loft" takes on a meaningful definition. The main condition was a separation of private and public areas that would refer to the location's industrial origins. Its high ceilings and regular shape led to the idea of inserting two gas tanks inside the space and turning them into bedroom and bathroom pods. The tanks contain the most intimate rooms of the residence, leaving the rest of the space free for the living area and kitchen. One of the modules, comprising two sleeping pods, is situated horizontally above the dining table and looks out over the living room and façade windows. The second tank, placed vertically from floor to ceiling, contains two bathrooms, one on top of the other. The lighting, the red furniture, and the blue floor add color that contrasts with the dominant gray tones.

Situé à New York, au quatrième étage d'un ancien parking du West Village, ce projet est l'exemple parfait du concept de « loft ». L'idée maîtresse consistait à créer une séparation entre le domaine privé et l'espace convivial, rappelant l'origine industrielle du site. La hauteur des plafonds et la régularité de la forme ont incité à intégrer à l'espace intérieur deux cuves à gaz et de les transformer en chambre à coucher et en salle de bains. Les sphères privées de la résidence sont installées dans ces cuves, ce qui libère l'espace restant pour les pièces à vivre et la cuisine. L'un des modules contenant deux chambres, est à l'horizontale au-dessus de la table et surplombe le salon et les fenêtres de façade. La deuxième cuve, à la verticale et tout en hauteur, abrite deux salles de bains – l'une au-dessus de l'autre. L'éclairage, le rouge des meubles et le bleu du sol sont autant de touches de couleurs qui tranchent sur la dominante grise de l'ensemble.

Dieses im vierten Stock eines ehemaligen Parkhauses in der West Village in New York gelegene Loft ist ein ausgezeichnetes Beispiel für ein Projekt, bei dem der Begriff „Loft" neu definiert wird. Die wichtigste Planungsvorgabe war die Trennung der privaten und öffentlichen Bereiche, die an den industriellen Ursprung erinnern sollten. Die hohe Decke und die gleichmäßige Form brachten die Gestalter auf die Idee, zwei Gastanks in den Raum einzubauen und für das Schlaf- und Badezimmer zu benutzen. Wohn- und Küchenbereich blieben offen. Eines der Module, bestehend aus zwei Schlafzonen, befindet sich horizontal über dem Esstisch, sodass man über das Wohnzimmer hinweg zum Fenster blickt. Der zweite Tank ist vertikal vom Boden zur Decke platziert und enthält zwei Bäder, die übereinander angeordnet sind. Die Beleuchtung, die roten Möbel und der blaue Fußboden setzen Farbtupfer in die von Grautönen dominierte Umgebung.

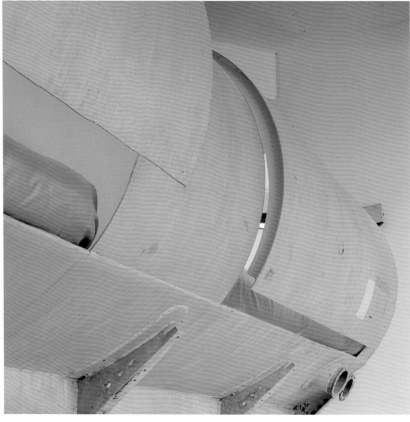

The insertion of gas tanks into a living space was a clever adaptation of industrial equipment to domestic use.

L'insertion de cuves à gaz à l'espace de vie est une façon judicieuse d'adapter le matériel industriel à l'usage domestique.

Das Einfügen der Gastanks in eine lebendige Umgebung stellt eine intelligente Verwendung von industriellen Gegenständen im Wohnbereich dar.

› Ground floor   Rez-de-chaussée   Erdgeschoss

› First floor   Premier étage   Erstes Obergeschoss

Steel and Glass

Johnson Chou
Toronto, Canada

To renovate this loft, the architect Johnson Chou began by removing all non-structural walls and introducing a large sandblasted screen to divide the main space. In addition, he layered the space with sliding partitions, such as the stainless-steel panel that separates the bedroom from the living area. In the bedroom, an aluminum-clad king-size bed cantilevered from the wall floats in front of floor-to-ceiling aluminum closets spanning the length of the room. The platform containing the bathroom areas is clad in blue-green slate and distinguished by a sculptural, free-standing stainless-steel vanity that heralds the passage into the washing areas. A massive white column contrasts with the smoothness of the steel and glass, whose constant presence lends a certain depth and warmth despite their cool starkness. A strip of clear glass along the bathroom door indulges the voyeur with a view of the sunken slate bath-tub from the living area.

Pour rénover ce loft, l'architecte Johnson Chou a commencé par éliminer tous les murs non porteurs, puis il a installé un grand écran poli au jet de sable pour diviser l'espace principal. A cela s'ajoutent des cloisons coulissantes qui scandent l'espace, comme le panneau en acier séparant la chambre de la pièce à vivre. Un immense lit recouvert d'aluminium, posé en can-tilever sur le mur, flotte devant des armoires d'aluminium qui couvrent toute la largeur et la hauteur de la chambre. La plate-forme, hébergeant l'espace salle de bains, est recouverte d'ardoise bleu-vert et mise en valeur par un plan de toilettes en inox, autoportante et sculptu-rale, en prélude à la salle d'eau. Une colonne blanche et massive tranche avec la délicatesse de l'acier et du verre dont l'omniprésence confère profondeur et chaleur malgré leur froide sobriété. Un filet de verre court le long de la porte de la salle de bains et permet un regard indiscret, depuis le salon, sur l'élégante baignoire installée au ras du sol.

Zur Umgestaltung dieses Lofts ließ der Architekt Johnson Chou zunächst alle nicht tragenden Wände entfernen und unterteilte den Raum durch einen großen, sandgestrahlten Schirm neu. Außerdem wurden gleitende Raumteiler wie Edelstahlplatten eingesetzt, die das Schlafzimmer vom Wohnzimmer trennen. Im Schlafzimmer schwebt ein freitragendes, riesiges Bett vor den deckenhohen Aluminiumschränken, die eine Seite des Raumes einnehmen. Die Plattform des Badezimmerbereiches ist mit blaugrünem Schiefer verkleidet. Der außergewöhnliche freiste-hende Toilettentisch aus Edelstahl steht am Übergang zum Waschbereich. Eine massive weiße Säule bildet einen Gegensatz zu dem glatten Stahl und dem Glas, die trotz ihrer Steife eine gewisse Tiefe und Wärme ausstrahlen. An der Badezimmertür befindet sich ein Glasstreifen, durch den man vom Wohnzimmer aus einen Blick auf die eingelassene Badewanne aus Schiefer erhaschen kann.

The electrical system provides maximum flexibility in the lighting while also contributing to the fluidity of the space.

Le système électrique permet de moduler au maximum l'éclairage tout en contribuant à la fluidité de l'espace.

Mit einem elektrischen System wurde eine sehr flexible Beleuchtung erzielt, durch die der Raum viel fließender wirkt.

› **Plan** Plan Grundriss

In the bedroom, an aluminum-clad king-size bed cantilevered from the wall floats in front of an expanse of floor-to-ceiling aluminum closets that span the length of the room.

Dans la chambre, un immense lit recouvert d'aluminium, posé en cantilever sur le mur, flotte devant les armoires d'aluminium qui couvrent toute la largeur et la hauteur de la pièce.

Im Schlafzimmer entspringt ein riesiges, mit Aluminium beschlagenes Bett freitragend der Wand und scheint vor den vom Boden bis zur Decke reichenden Wandschränken, die die gesamte Länge des Raumes einnehmen, zu schweben.

The materials used for the bathroom elements are characterized by their purity and simplicity.

Les matériaux définissant les éléments de la salle de bains sont empreints de pureté et de simplicité.

Im Badezimmer wurden sehr einfache und reine Materialien eingesetzt.

The sunken bathtub is glimpsed from the living area through a 10-inch strip of clear glass running along the bathroom door.

Une bande de verre de 25 cm, le long de la porte de la salle de bains, permet un regard indiscret depuis le salon.

Vom Wohnbereich aus erhascht man durch den 25 cm breiten, durchsichtigen Glasstreifen an der Badezimmertür einen Blick auf die eingelassene Badewanne.

Photo Credits   Crédits photographiques   Fotonachweis